ISLAMIC BANKING AND FINANCE

ISLAMIC BANKING AND FINANCE

By

Ismail Thamarasseri
Assistant Professor
Department of Education
Central University of Kashmir
Srinagar - 190 004
(J&K) (INDIA)

&

Abdul Rahiman A.T
Assistant Professor
Department of Commerce
Farook Arts & Science College Kottakkal
Malappuram - 676 503
Dt., Kerala (INDIA)

DPH

DISCOVERY PUBLISHING HOUSE PVT. LTD.
NEW DELHI-110 002

Published by:
Tilak Wasan
DISCOVERY PUBLISHING HOUSE PVT. LTD.
4383/4B, Ansari Road, Darya Ganj
New Delhi-110 002 (India)
Phone : +91-11-23279245, 43596064-65
Fax : +91-11-23253475
E-mail : discoverypublishinghouse@gmail.com
sales@discoverypublishinggroup.com
parul.wasan@gmail.com
web : www.discoverypublishinggroup.com

***First Edition:* 2014**

ISBN: 978-93-5056-453-0

Islamic Banking and Finance

Printed at:
Dynamic Printers
Delhi

Preface

Interest free banking has been defined as banking in consonance with the ethos and value system of Islam and governed, in addition to the conventional good governance and risk management rules, by the principles laid down by Islamic Shariah. Interest free banking is a narrow concept denoting a number of banking instruments or operations, which avoid interest. Islamic banking, the more general term is expected not only to avoid interest-based transactions, prohibited in the Islamic Shariah, but also to avoid unethical practices and participate actively in achieving the goals and objectives of a right economy. Islamic Banking is a part of the economic system and activities of a society that wants total fairness to its members through delivery of social justice, construction and development, employment for all etc. As such Islamic banking may be considered the engine in a vehicle but not the whole vehicle and thus Islamic banking principles extend beyond the fact that its banking activities prohibits interest as we all commonly know. The principal differentiation factor of Islamic banking institutions rests with the fact that they are multi disciplined banking organizations acting as commercial and specialised banking institutions at the same time and that they are not credit provider since they are neither creditors nor debtors, and do not transact in interest give or take.

Islamic Economics and Finance, the growing area thought and practice now a days in all over the world. Many Indian banking institutions also turn to this dimension. Lack of reference/study materials and research studies felt in this area. This book has been mainly designed to serve the requirements of the students of Islamic Economics and Finance. Also this book is highly useful for those who interested in this area.

First and for most we would like to thank and praise the God, the Almighty, for making we capable to complete the work successfully. The authors extremely indebted to Mr. Muhammed Palath, Head, Department of Post Graduate Diploma In Islamic Economics and Finance (PGDIEF) Al Jamia, Santhapuram and Faculty members of Islamic Economics And Finance, Al Jamia Al Islamiya, Santhapuram, Malappuram, Kerala.

In preparation of this book the authors had to refer to the works of other authors and information sources. The authors feel a deep sense of gratitude for incorporating their ideas in the text. The authors extremely indebted to various authors, editors, educationists, technologists and research scholars, whose views and opinions have been incorporated in this book. The authors grateful to their colleagues, friends, family members and students whose offered suggestions, guidance and assistance. Finally, the authors whole heartedly expresses their indebtedness to M/s. Discovery Publishing House Pvt. Ltd., New Delhi for the meticulous process and publishing of the work. Moreover, all the suggestions and comments are invited for the further improvement of the work.

Ismail Thamarasseri
Abdul Rahiman A.T

Contents

Preface

1. **Islamic Finance a Solution for Global Economic Crisis** **1**
   An Introduction
2. **Global Financial Recession** **4**
   What Is Recession?; Recession-Definition; Recession and it's Attributes; History and Evolution; The Great Depression in 1930; Recession in 2000s; The Financial Crisis of 2007-10 – The Present Situation; Some Charecteristics of a Recession; The Important Global Economic Crisis At a Glance Session 1920's; Root of the Current Global Financial Crisis; The after Effect of Crisis in United States and Other Advanced Economies.
3. **Islamic Finance** **23**
   Search for a New World Order
   What is Islamic Finance?; Definitions of Islamic Economics; Religious History of Islamic Economics; The Five Prohibitions in Financial Activities in Islam; The Important Principles of Islamic Finance; Interest Free Element in Islamic Finance; Development and Present Condition; Impact on Western Financial Markets; The Profit and Loss Sharing Principle (PLSP).

4. How Islamic Finance as a Solution for Global Financial Crisis **42**

Primary Cause of the Crises; The Collapse of Long-term Capital Management; The Prevailing Imbalances in the U.S. Economy; Justification for Islamic Financial System-Under Economic Crisis.

5. Islamic Law of Contracts **53**

Historical Evolution of Contract in Islamic Law; Essential Elements of a Valid Contract; Classification of Contract; Reflection and Overview on the Classifications of Contracts; Contracts of Exchange (Mu'awadat); Contracts of Utilisation of Usufruct ('Uqud al-Manfa'at); Contract of Ijarah (Transfer of Usufruct for a Consideration); Contracts of Security.

6. Islamic Fund and Asset Management **73**

Shariah Compliant Equity Funds; Islamic Unit Trusts; Shari'ah Principles for Investment Funds; Islamic Funds and Socially Responsible Investments; Proposed Additional Requirements for Islamic Unit Trust Funds; Islamic Indexes for Islamic Funds.

7. Sukuk **89**

Islamic Equivalent of Bond

Basics of Sukuk; Role of Sharia Advisors in Sukuk; Sukuk in the Context of UK and Europe; Model of a Classic Sukuk Structure; Increasing Interest; Eligible Assets; Enforceability; The Future; Islamic Bonds (Sukuk): Its Introduction and Application; Benefits and Features; Types of Sukuk; Mudaraba Sukuk in Practice; Musharaka Sukuk in Practice; Features of Ijarah Sukuk; Ijara Sukuk in Practice; Murabaha Sukuk in Practice; Salam Sukuk in Practice; Istisna Sukuk in Practice; Hybrid Sukuk in Practice; Conclusion.

8. Venture Capital **120**

History; Origins of Modern Private Equity; Early Venture Capital and the Growth of Silicon Valley; Venture Capital in the 1980s; The Venture Capital Boom and the Internet Bubble (1995 to 2000); The Bursting of the Internet Bubble and the Private Equity Crash (2000-03); Structure of Venture Capital

Firms; Types of Venture Capital Firms; Roles within Venture Capital Firms; Structure of the Funds; Compensation; Venture Capital Funding; Main Alternatives to Venture Capital; The Establishment of the VC Sector in the Islamic World; Models and Acceptable Structures for Islamic; Venture Capital; Conventional Venture Capital Practice Shari'ah View (Ahmed H., 2004); Structuring Issues; Upsurge of Islamic Syndicated Financing.

9. Shariah Supervision in Modern Islamic Finance **145**

What is Shariah Supervision?; Purpose; Background; Elements of Shari'ah Supervision: Numbers; Elements of Shari'ah Supervision: Qualifications; Elements of Shari'ah Supervision: Independence; Elements of Shari'ah Supervision: Communication; Elements of Shari'ah Supervision: Education; Shari'ah Supervision Then and Now, The Importance of Shariah Supervision in Islamic Financial Institutions; Issues Relating to the Working of SSBs; Role of Central Banks and Regulatory Bodies.

10. Micro-finance **160**

The Challenge; Boundaries and Principles; Debates at the Boundaries; Financial Needs of Poor People; Ways in which Poor People Manage their Money; Current Scale of Micro-finance Operations; 'Inclusive Financial Systems'; Informal Financial Service Providers; Member-owned Organizations; NGOs; Formal Financial Institutions; Micro-credit and the Web; Evidence for Reducing Poverty; Micro-finance and Social Interventions; Other Criticisms.

Bibliography ***175***

Index ***181***

CHAPTER

1

Islamic Finance a Solution for Global Economic Crisis

An Introduction

Throughout this crisis that has so consumed the attention of the world in recent we have watched with grave concern as it cascaded outwards from the sectors originally affected. Alan Greenspan recently called it a 'once-in-a-century credit tsunami', born of a collapse deep inside the US housing sector. But metaphors from other recent disasters come to mind too, as we have watched this great wave over top one economic levee after another. Instability has surged from sector to sector, first from housing into banking and other financial markets, and then on into all parts of the real economy. The crisis has surged across the public-private boundary, as the hit to private firms' balance sheets has now imposed heavy new demands on the public sector's finances. It has surged across national borders within the developed world, as the people of United States know all too well. And now there are reasons to fear that the crisis will swamp emerging markets and other developing countries, cutting into the considerable economic progress of recent years.

The financial system has decidedly played an active role in the accelerated development of the world economy, particularly after the Second World War. An unending stream of financial innovations, including the revolution in information and communications technology, has played a crucial role in this development. The system is, however, now plagued by persistent crisis. According to one estimate, there have been more than 100 crisis over the last four decade.

Not a single geographical area or major country has been spared the effect of these crisis. Even some of the countries that have generally followed sound fiscal and monetary policies have become engulfed in these crisis. The prevailing financial crisis, which started in the summer of 2007, is more severe than any in the past and shows no sign of abating despite a coordinated bail out of three to four trillion dollars by the US, the UK, Europe and a number of other countries. It has seized-up money markets and led to a precipitous decline in property and stock values, bank failures, and nervous anxiety about the fate of the global economy and the financial system.

This has created an uneasy feeling that there is something basically wrong with the system. There is, hence, a call for a new architecture. The new architecture demands an innovation that could help prevent the outbreak and spread of crisis or, at least, minimize their frequency and severity. Since a number of the crisis experienced around the world are generally of a serious nature and have been recurring persistently, cosmetic changes in the existing system may not be sufficient. It is necessary to have an innovation that would be really effective. It may not be possible to figure out such an innovation without first determining the primary cause of the crisis.

Even in the modern world, where the financial idiologies are controlling the foremost of activities in human life in the world. The economic pholosophies (Socrates, Plato, Socialism, Communism, Marshel's economic thought, etc.), has been introduced and followed in the previous civilizations, the previous thoughts are couldn't act as a full-fledged economic thought for Global Economic Recession.

Global financial crisis which hit many too-big-too-fail countries and financial institution in the world was mainly made happen by debt securitisation. Derivative instruments resulted from this process obviously were not backed by real asset. When any party came up with investment on these instruments, the investment would never support the development of real sector economy, instead, it just worsen the situation by creating bubble economic. This condition becomes more harmful when the securitised debts default. This practice is strictly forbidden according to Islamic finance principles. It has inherent risk management tools to prevent the crisis.

In this the special dilemma the economic world is reached increase the relevence of a efficient and equitable option for recuperating the present special situation. Now the Islamic Finance provide the better option. Islamic Finance have it's own practical philosaphies against any crisis. Here, this project attempts to examine the root of the financial crisis and find the solution from Islamic finance principles.

CHAPTER

2

Global Financial Recession

What Is Recession?

A financial crisis is a disturbance to financial markets that disrupts the market's capacity to allocate capital – financial intermediation and hence investment come to a halt.

Investors should take risks, and risks mean that some proportion of investments will fail. This is why we have domestic bankruptcy laws that provide for orderly workouts when investments and the firms that made them do fail. Similarly, if the international capital markets are functioning well, mistakes will be made. Then one or another country (or its private sector borrowers) will fail: a crisis. History records many. We should not expect or even wish to prevent them all. That would be at the cost of insufficient, excessively risk-averse investment. So such crises will always recur – but capital markets forget.

The term 'financial crisis' is used too loosely, often to denote either a banking crisis, or a debt crisis, or a foreign exchange market crisis. It is perhaps preferable to invoke it only for the 'big one': a generalised, international financial crisis. This is a nexus of foreign exchange market disturbances, debt defaults (sovereign or private), and banking system failures: a triple crisis, in which the interactions are the key to causality, depth, and persistence (Eichengreen and Portes, 1987).

The widespread securitisation of debt in recent years has not changed the picture – after all, one of the major historical examples is the 1930s crisis of defaults on sovereign bonds. Nor has it diminished the importance of banking sector fragility in provoking and exacerbating financial crisis.

All crisis are 'crisis of success' (Portes and Vines, 1997). The initial capital inflow that ultimately proves unsustainable (and perhaps unprofitable) is both a sign and – for a time – a cause of economic promise and success. But we have not yet learned how best to cope with the capital inflows, so success may lead to failure.

All crisis raise the problem of distinguishing between insolvency and illiquidity. Today, some say that the 'Asian miracle' economies are actually 'hollowed out', 'zombie' economies: all that investment just went into creating excess capacity or driving up real estate prices. Others argue that the growth was real, that these economies should still come top in the World Competitiveness Report, and their problem is simply overvalued exchange rates and the classical 'run' – a self-fulfilling crisis of liquidation of short-term loans. We will not know for some time which view is correct.

Because crisis will always recur and because their causation is so complex, we shall never arrive at an international financial system – whatever its 'architecture' that can dispense with mechanisms for the resolution of financial crises. 'Better information', 'early warning' and 'preventive measures' will not remove the need for orderly workouts, whatever the source(s) of the crisis.

Many professionals and experts around the world believe that a true economic recession can only be confirmed if GDP (Gross Domestic Product) growth is negative for a period of two or more consecutive quarters.

The roots of a recession and its true starting point actually rest in the several quarters of positive but slowing growth before the recession cycle really begins. Often in a mild recession the first quarter of negative growth is followed by slight positive growth, then negative growth returns and the recession trend continues.

While the 'two quarter' definition is accepted globally, many economists have trouble supporting it completely as it does not consider other important economic change variables. For instance, current national unemployment rates or consumer confidence and spending levels are all a part of the economic system and must to be taken into account when defining a recession and its attributes.

The agency that is officially in charge of declaring a recession in the United States is known as the National Bureau of Economic Research, or NBER. The NBER define's a recession as a *'significant decline in economic activity lasting more than a few months'*.

We often do not receive official word of an economic recession until we are several months into it as NBER must take time to calculate the multitude of variables available before making their decision. While economic recessions are foreseeable, they generally are not detected until already in motion.

It is actually more common than we might realise for countries around the world to experience mild economic recessions. Recession (or contraction) is a natural result of the economic cycle and will adjust for changes in consumer spending and consumption or increasing and decreasing prices of goods and labour.

Rarely though entirely possible, experiencing a multitude of these negative factors simultaneously can lead to a deep recession or even long economic depression.

Recession-Definition

According to the Business Cycle Dating Committee of the National Bureau of Economic Research (NBER), USA, recession is defined as *"a significant decline in economic activity spread across the economy, lasting more than a few months, normally visible in real gross product (GDP), real income, employment, industrial production and wholesale-retail sales"*

In a 1975 *New York Times* article, economic statistician Julius Shiskin suggested several rules of thumb for defining a recession, one of which was *'two down quarters of GDP'*. In time, the other rules of thumb were forgotten, and a recession is now often defined simply as a period when GDP falls (negative real economic growth) for at least two quarters. Some economists prefer a definition of a 1.5 per cent rise in unemployment within 12 months.

Recession and it's Attributes

In economics, a recession is a business cycle contraction, a general slowdown in economic activity over a period of time. During recessions, many macroeconomic indicators vary in a similar way. Production as measured by Gross Domestic Product (GDP), employment, investment spending, capacity utilisation, household incomes, business profits and inflation all fall during recessions; while bankruptcies and the unemployment rate rise.

Recessions are generally believed to be caused by a widespread drop in spending. Governments usually respond to recessions by adopting expansionary macroeconomic policies, such as increasing money supply, increasing government spending and decreasing taxation.

Attributes

A recession has many attributes that can occur simultaneously and includes declines in component measures of economic activity (GDP) such as consumption, investment, government spending, and net export activity. These summary measures reflect underlying drivers such as employment levels and skills, household savings rates, corporate investment decisions, interest rates, demographics, and government policies.

Economist Richard Koo wrote that under ideal conditions, a country's economy should have the household sector as net savers and the corporate sector as net borrowers, with the government budget nearly balanced and net exports near zero. When these relationships become imbalanced, recession can develop within the country or create pressure for recession in another country. Policy responses are often designed to drive the economy back towards this ideal state of balance.

A severe (GDP down by 10%) or prolonged (three or four years) recession is referred to as an economic depression, although some argue that their causes and cures can be different. As an informal short-hand, economists sometimes refer to different recession shapes, such as V-shaped, U-shaped, L-shaped and W-shaped recessions.

In the US, V-shaped, or short-and-sharp contractions followed by rapid and sustained recovery, occurred in 1954 and 1990-91; U-shaped (prolonged slump) in 1974-75, and W-shaped, or double-dip recessions in 1949 and 1980-82. Japan's 1993-94 recession was U-shaped and its 8-out-of-9 quarters of contraction in 1997-99 can be described as L-shaped. Korea, Hong Kong and South-east Asia experienced U-shaped recessions in 1997-98, although Thailand's eight consecutive quarters of decline should be termed L-shaped.

Recessions have psychological and confidence aspects. For example, if the expectation develops that economic activity will slow, firms may decide to reduce employment levels and save money rather than invest. Such expectations can create a self-reinforcing downward cycle, bringing about or worsening a recession.

History and Evolution

"The credit and capital markets have grown too rapidly, with too little transparency and accountability. Prepare for an explosion that will rock the western financial system to its foundation". (Barberton and Lane (1999).

As mentioned by Barberto and Lane (1999), the explosion just became a reality. Though the crises in the US and Europe were one of the crises series which regularly hit the world starting from the 20th century, most economists view that the current financial crisis is the greatest one that beat the world economy, even if compared with the Great Depression in 1930s.

Since current global financial crisis is frightened can bring prolonged period of economy down turn, it is very important to find ways to cure it. However, as always done by a doctor before giving medical treatment to his patients, it is important for us to firstly observe the ground of the problem.

The Great Depression in 1930

The Great Depression was a severe worldwide economic depression in the decade preceding World War II. The timing of the Great Depression varied across nations, but in most countries it started in about 1929 and lasted until the late 1930s or early 1940s. It was the longest, most widespread, and deepest depression of the 20th century, and is used in the 21st century as an example of how far the world's economy can decline. The depression originated in the United States, starting with the stock market crash of October 29, 1929 (known as Black Tuesday), but quickly spread to almost every country in the world.

The Great Depression had devastating effects in virtually every country, rich and poor. Personal income, tax revenue, profits and prices dropped, and international trade plunged by a half to two-thirds. Unemployment in the United States rose to 25 per cent, and in some countries rose as high as 33 per cent. Cities all around the world were hit hard, especially those dependent on heavy industry. Construction was virtually halted in many countries. Farming and rural areas suffered as crop prices fell by approximately 60 per cent. Facing plummeting demand with few alternate sources of jobs, areas dependent on primary sector industries such as cash cropping, mining and logging suffered the most.

Countries started to recover by the mid-1930s, but in many countries the negative effects of the Great Depression lasted until the start of World War II.

Recession in 2000s

The late-2000s recession (or sometimes the *Great Recession*) is an economic recession that began in the United States in December 2007 (and with much greater intensity since September 2008, according to the National Bureau of Economic Research). It spread to much of the industrialised world, and has caused a pronounced deceleration of economic activity. This global recession has been taking place in an economic environment characterised by various imbalances and was sparked by the outbreak of the financial crisis of 2007-10.

Although the late-2000s recession has at times been referred to as 'the Great Recession', this same phrase has been used to refer to every recession of the several preceding decades. In July 2009, it was announced that a growing number of economists believed that the recession may have ended.

The financial crisis has been linked to reckless and unsustainable lending practices compounded by government intervention and the growing trend of securitisation of real estate mortgages in the United States. The US mortgage-backed securities, which had risks that were hard to assess, were marketed around the world. A more broad based credit boom fed a global speculative bubble in real estate and equities, which served to reinforce the risky lending practices. The precarious financial situation was made more difficult by a sharp increase in oil and food prices. The emergence of Sub-prime loan losses in 2007 began the crisis and exposed other risky loans and over-inflated asset prices. With loan losses mounting and the fall of Lehman Brothers on September 15, 2008, a major panic broke out on the inter-bank loan market. As share and housing prices declined, many large and well established investment and commercial banks in the United States and Europe suffered huge losses and even faced bankruptcy, resulting in massive public financial assistance.

The Financial Crisis of 2007-10 – The Present Situation

The financial crisis of 2007 to the present is a crisis triggered by a liquidity crisis in the United States banking system and caused by the overvaluation of assets. It has resulted in the collapse of large financial institutions, the bailout of banks by national governments and downturns in stock markets around the world. In many areas, the housing market has also suffered, resulting in numerous evictions, foreclosures and prolonged vacancies. It is considered by many economists to be the worst financial crisis since the Great Depression of the 1930s. It contributed to the failure of key businesses, declines in consumer wealth estimated in the trillions of U.S., dollars, substantial financial commitments incurred by governments, and a significant decline in economic activity. Many causes have been suggested, with varying weight assigned by experts. Both market-based and regulatory solutions have been implemented or are under consideration, while significant risks remain for the world economy over the 2010-11 periods.

The collapse of a global housing bubble, which peaked in the U.S., in 2006, caused the values of securities tied to real estate pricing to plummet thereafter, damaging financial institutions globally. Questions regarding bank solvency, declines in credit availability, and damaged investor confidence had an impact on global stock markets, where securities suffered large losses during late 2008 and early 2009. Economies worldwide slowed during this period as credit tightened and international trade declined. Critics argued that credit rating agencies and investors failed to accurately price the risk involved with mortgage-related financial products, and that governments did not adjust their regulatory practices to address 21st century financial markets. Governments and central banks responded with unprecedented fiscal stimulus, monetary policy expansion, and institutional bailouts.

The outlines of the financial and credit crisis are clear though the blame will be argued and discussed far into the future. Three primary causes played out over the past decade culminating in the tumultuous events of the past three years with the American Federal Government on putting forth a plan to buy the housing based bad debt of the entire United States financial system.

In the early part of this decade the Federal Reserve held interest rates at historically low levels for three years. In the mortgage industry increasingly lax credit standards were encouraged by government pressure to lend to marginal customers. Finally Wall Street firms became enamored of the profitability and supposed safety of their securitised credit derivative instruments, not only originating many products but also stocking their balance sheets with them.

In the aftermath of the 9/11 attacks in 2001 the Federal Reserve cut the Fed Funds rate in half, to 1.75 per cent. The rate would stay below 2.0 per cent for almost three years. Those low nominal rates, negative in real inflation adjusted terms, stoked a building and buying boom in housing that developed into a huge speculative bubble.

When the Fed brought rates back to 5.25 per cent at the end of June 2006, the bubble began to deflate; the housing based credit crisis began a little more than a year later. Market bubbles always burst. Perhaps the fall of the housing market now seems preordained. But at the time the risk of the dicey mortgages spread throughout the financial system was disguised by the financially engineered instruments that had repackaged the questionable bits with higher quality debt, supposedly insuring the whole against default.

Starting in the closing years of the Clinton Administration the Community Redevelopment Act, a Carter Era programme, was used to force banks to lend to mortgage customers formerly considered ineligible for loans. In pursuit of a social goal, universal home ownership, banks either lowered credit standards and granted mortgages or faced fines and business penalties for 'redlining'. Banks by and large complied with government dictates.

Two of the government sponsored enterprises (GSEs) in the mortgage field, the Federal National Mortgage Association (Fannie Mae) and the Federal Home Loan Mortgage Corporation (Freddie Mac) bought much of the bank mortgage debt and sold it back to the market with their implied government guarantee behind it. The banks and loan companies used the cash obtained to sponsor more loans and keep the housing bubble inflating. As with the banks, the GSEs also brought some of this debt onto their balance sheets. All in all these two GSEs held title to or guaranteed upwards of 70 per cent of residential mortgages in the United States. Their mortgage paper is endemic on the balance sheets of the world's financial institutions.

The nozzle through which much of the air inflating the housing bubble passed was the asset backed collateralized debt obligation (CDO) fashioned by Wall Street's leading investment houses and banks. Combining different types and grades of debt in one instrument these complex securities were supposed to reduce risk of the whole below the level of the individual pieces. Their complexity often rendered them opaque to the rating agencies whose rankings customers buying the securities relied on for risk measurement. Usually sold with default insurance these securities had one major flaw, their balance sheet value was assessed not by the value of the underlying income streams but by their sale price in the secondary market. If there were no market, if no one were willing to buy these securities, the theoretical book value fell to zero.

As the housing market stagnated and then fell, the value of those securities with housing components dropped as default rates on mortgages rose. But housing prices in the US have only declined on average about 20 per cent. How could such a large but not catastrophic decline threaten the very foundations of the financial system? The crux is the mark to market nature of the security. As the financial markets progressively lost faith in asset backed securities and as housing prices continued to fall bids for these securities became scarce. The lower the prices for the securities the more capital the firm had to set aside to meet regulatory limits. The firms that owned large amounts of these securities were caught in a downward spiral of devalued securities requiring ever large amounts of the firms capital for support which progressively undermined the worth of the firms stock and market confidence in the firm's solvency which in turn demanded more capital support.

The United States has had market bubbles before, but none shook the financial system to its core and threatened the financial system. What has been different this time? The factor that levered a serious housing market bubble and collapse into a threat to the entire US and indeed world financial system was the asset-backed derivative. These new and poorly understood instruments were embraced by the financial world for their touted safety and for their high return. Yet their safety, the quality of their financial analysis and most importantly the underlying assumptions were completely untested.

Chief among the assumptions underpinning these derivative securities was the mark to market rule for valuation. Imposed by regulators in the aftermath of the failure of Enron it posits, natural enough in normal times, a functioning secondary market. Its purpose was to insure realistic pricing for securities. All is fine with the rule unless there is no market. As with the failure of Long-Term Credit, it was the assumption that there will always be a functioning orderly market that was at fault. Markets are not always rational, they are voluntary and they are psychological. People and firms do not have to participate. When enough market participants choose abstinence the market collapses and all calculations that depend on market pricing are void.

Markets are reflections of the faith and credit of their participants. When that is lost no amount of financial engineering can make up for the loss of liquidity. In a panic the market vanishes. The asset backed derivative made the stability of the entire financial system beholden to its least stable component, the psychology of the market.

Some Charecteristics of a Recession

- Declining demand for output leading to higher levels of spare productive cappacity.
- Contracting employment/rising unemployment as firms lay-off workersto control their costs.
- A sharp fall in business confidence and profit.
- A decrease in fixed capital investment spending because there is insufficient demand to justify new capital projects.
- De-stocking and heavy price discounting – this leads to lower inflation.
- Reduced inflationary pressure in the labour market as unemployment rises.

- Falling demand for imports.
- Increased government borrowing.

The Important Global Economic Crisis – At a Glance Session 1920's

A prosperous decade for many. Americans speculated wildly on stocks, over extending themselves by buying securities 'on margin' (*i.e.,* credit). So many shares had been bought on margin, that much of it amounted to little more that paper.

As production soared, consumer spending power failed to keep pace. The result was overproduction. Goods piled up and prices fell, industry began laying off workers. As more workers were laid off, the market place grew smaller and smaller.

1929 Stock Market Crash

The crash came about due to careless credit based investment and increased industrial output in a shrinking market for industrial goods. After 1929 recession followed.

1930's The Great Depression

Global economies collapse. Many countries face hunger and poverty.

1970s' Oil Crisis, Stagflation and Vietnam

The 70s was the era of stagflation, with 12 per cent inflation requiring higher interest rates and cuts in government spending. Unemployment hit 9 per cent in a recession lasting 16 months between 1973 and 1975.

1980's Rcession

A recession occurred at the start of Ronald Reagan's presidency (US), when the chairman of the Fed, Paul Volcker, was determined to beat inflation once and for all. Interest rates rose to almost 20 per cent, turning large chunks of America's industrial heartland into a rustbelt.

October 19th 1987 – Black Monday

The largest single day drop in the Dow Jones Industrial Average index.

2001-9/11 The September 11th Attack (US), and the trade, commercial crisis followed by the incident.

Root of the Current Global Financial Crisis

The Bank for International Settlement (BIS) has mentioned on its 2008 annual report that the root of almost all crises has been excessive and imprudent lending by banks. Furthermore, this factor also becomes important cause that makes this current crisis happen, which was boomed with defaults of subprime mortgages in the United States on 7th February 2007 (Sakti, 2009).

The default was made happen by excessive and imprudent mortgage lending given by Washington Mutual to many high-risk home purchasers in the US. In return, the purchasers should pay certain amount of service fees to Mutual. This mortgage lending was then securitised by the Mutual and sold to mortgage guarantee institutions (Fannie Mae and Freddie Mac) to earn more funds. Furthermore, the guarantors pooled and packaged the mortgages into instrument called Mortgage backed Securities (MBS). This type of instrument later sold to the Wall Street. After that, the Wall Street re-packaged the MBS into another derivative instrument called as Collateralized Debt Obligations (CDOs) and sold them to some investment banks, *e.g.* Lehman Brothers (Karim, 2009). From this stage, the investment banks sold the instruments by mixing prime and subprime debt to pass the entire risk of default of even subprime debt from mortgage originators to the ultimate purchasers who would have normally been reluctant to bear such a risk. But do to this camouflage packaging; the buyers could not clearly see the inherent risk of the financial instrument they bought. As a result, the lending to subprime borrowers and speculators increased steeply (Chapra, 2008).

Those unhealthy practices lead to nationalizations of a number of banks by the governments in the US, the UK, Europe and a number of other countries. In consequence, the creditors became uncertain with the situations and sought for protection against default by buying derivatives like

Credit Default Swaps (CDSs). By owning these instruments, they pay a premium to hedge funds for the compensation they will receive in case the debtor defaults. Another problem here is that the hedge funds did not only sell the CDSs to creditors, instead, they also sell the derivatives to a large number of others who were willing to bet on the default of the debtor. They even resold the swaps to others. Consequently, the hedge funds as well as the investment banks could not afford to pay such incentives to the instrument buyers. Such default, therefore, brought those institutions to unavoidable bankruptcy and those buyers to extremely high investment losses.

The after Effect of Crisis in United States and Other Advanced Economies

The basic contours of the current financial crisis are by now well known. As the well-known economist Herbert Stein once pointed out, if something cannot go on forever, it won't. Annual double-digit increases in US housing prices proved unsustainable, and the rapidly growing price-rent and price-income ratios clearly had to fall. The first clear sign that the US housing bubble was bursting, the mid-2007 crisis in the sub-prime mortgage market (stemming from the significant increase in defaults), transmitted losses to a whole set of securitised financial products such as mortgage-backed securities. Many of these new securitised financial products with layers of underlying assets were revealed to be far riskier than their credit ratings indicated. The drop in value of these assets dealt a blow to the balance sheets of many financial institutions. Even worse, the financial innovations of this decade – many of which had been sold on the promise that they would diversify and minimize risk – turned out to be transmission mechanisms for instability. The sub-prime mortgage crisis thus became a full-fledged financial crisis, which in turn has led to a collapse in equity markets.

Although the full-fledged crisis struck first in the United States, the US is not alone in its vulnerability to shocks and collapses in consumer confidence. Many countries, both developed and emerging-market, have recently experienced bubbles in asset markets. Housing prices have risen rapidly for reasons not entirely explained by fundamentals in such countries as Ireland, the UK, and Australia, according to the IMF (2008), while countries like China and Russia saw speculative frenzy drive their equity markets to dizzying heights before the crisis. Financial integration and cross-border holdings of mutual funds, hedge funds, developed-country bank subsidiaries, and insurance companies have transmitted turbulence and helped propagate asset price collapses in European and other countries.

The bursting of a bubble this large, with the financial consequences that we have seen in recent weeks for credit and equity markets, makes a recession inevitable in the United States and likely in other developed economies. Indeed, job losses and other indicators suggest that the US has probably already entered a recession, and the IMF and World Bank are currently projecting 2009 growth in the US of just 0.1 to 0.2 per cent (International Monetary Fund 2008; World Bank Forthcoming). Growth in the Euro area and Japan will also decline sharply, with the IMF predicting 2009 GDP growth of just 0.2 and 0.5 per cent, respectively, and the latest World Bank projections even more pessimistic. More recent private sector forecasts are at least as gloomy, and in some cases much more so. (Berner 2008; Martin and Schaffler 2008).

What makes the recession a macroeconomic certainty is that the United States must undergo adjustment to redress the imbalances of the bubble years 6. Fortunately, when the crisis burst into the open after September 14th and the bankruptcy of Lehman Brothers, policy-makers acted swiftly and pragmatically to avoid the worst consequences – a complete shutdown of the global inter-bank market, a rapid credit crunch, and its eventual consequence, the collapse of the global banking system. Thanks to the comprehensive, decisive, and co-ordinated intervention by Euro Zone, UK, Japanese, and US authorities in the first week of October, there are reasons to hope that the collapse of the banking sector can be prevented. But the catalyst of the banking crisis – the collapse of the US housing bubble – cannot be reversed. The extent of the meltdown goes far beyond the estimated $1.3 trillion in sub-prime mortgages at the start of the crisis. The housing price collapse of 2007-08 and more recent meltdown in equities have dealt US homeowners trillions of dollars in capital losses – an estimated $2.4 trillion in just the nine months through June 2008 (Federal Reserve figures, cited in World Bank Forthcoming), and much more with the recent plunge in stock markets. Losses of this magnitude will likely have significant wealth effects on consumption. Furthermore, and perhaps even more important, many households will be constrained by no longer being able to borrow against their home equity. This will lead to a fall in consumption and increase in saving, as households adjust to their new circumstances. US homeowners will no longer be able to count on rapid price increases that will allow them to downsize homes after retirement and live off the capital gains. Instead, they will need to become more cautious in consumption and to save more of their current income. In addition, losses from 401K pension-schemes and in stocks are likely to increase savings propensity by US households. Predicting the magnitude of these effects is challenging, because they depend in part on consumers' perceptions of the crisis and their psychology. But the concurrence of historically large collapses in multiple asset markets, together with bad economic news on other fronts, makes it hard to be sanguine about consumption growth.

Moreover, the data suggest little reason to hope for a quick rebound in housing prices. Based on historical ratios between housing prices and such variables as rents, income, or the economy's overall price index, it appears that US housing prices could fall another 10 per cent or more before reaching their long-run equilibrium level. And if Irrational pessimism replaces irrational exuberance, prices could compound the damage by overshooting on the way down. Similar dynamics could play out in other countries that had apparently larger housing price gaps than the United States at the end of 2007 – such as the United Kingdom and France, as well as a number of smaller economies (International Monetary Fund 2008). Large price declines in these other markets would exacerbate the global wealth effects.

The Effects on Developing Countries

What will be the likely effects on developing countries? One effect will be a Substantial reduction in their exports, as the rapid pace of trade expansion of this decade decelerates sharply. The IMF recently projected growth in world trade volumes of just 4.1 per cent in 2009, down from 9.3 per cent as recently as 2006; in our own more recent projections, the deceleration is much more rapid and could in fact lead trade volumes to fall in 2009 (World bank Forthcoming). While the fall in export volume growth is projected to be greater for advanced economies than for developing economies, the latter may also suffer more from declines in the terms of trade – especially in the case of commodity exporters, given that we expect non-oil commodity prices to fall by perhaps one-fifth in 2009.

In addition, the crisis will deal a negative shock to investment in emerging markets. All of the main external sources of funds for investment are likely to drop off sharply in the first round of effects. Portfolio investment will fall, as greater risk aversion keeps capital closer to home. While FDI is historically more resilient to shocks, it too is expected to decline. In addition, developing countries that are able to gain access to capital will pay higher interest rates, because of the flight to safety and greater risk aversion of lenders. As noted above, the global slowdown will reduce demand for commodities and manufactured goods, cutting into export earnings. And as labour markets slacken, foreign workers are likely to suffer disproportionate impacts on their earnings, which will reduce remittances. About half of all developing countries have been running current account deficits of 5 per cent of GDP or more, and in some cases the deficits are around 10 per cent. These economies will be highly vulnerable to swings in these various sources in external financing.

Overall, we now expect investment in middle-income countries in 2009 to grow at less than half the 2007 rate of 13 per cent.

Second round effects will likely deepen the slowdown. Because of the investment surge of the past five years, an especially large number of investment projects are already underway. As investment financing drops off, two outcomes are possible, neither of them attractive. In some cases, the projects will not be completed, making them unproductive and saddling banks' balance sheets with non-performing loans. In other cases, when the projects are completed, they will add to the excess production capacity that will result from the global slowdown, and thereby add to the risk of deflation.

As a result of all these factors, we now expect that developing countries' collective GDP growth will decline to less than 5 per cent, compared with an average of more than 7 per cent in 2004-07. Moreover, the effects on developing countries may not be limited to a drop in investment and export earnings and a slowdown of GDP growth. There is a distinct danger that emerging markets could go through crises of their own, for example if their own domestic asset-market bubbles burst (or even if fair-market values collapse) and weaken their own banking sectors. Sharp drops in stock markets in developing countries have already signaled investors' concerns about the medium-term future, and the decline in portfolio values may also have substantial wealth effects on consumption, exacerbating the effects of the slowdown. Countries with high balance-of-payments and fiscal deficits will be especially vulnerable. What will exacerbate the troubles of developing economies is the simultaneous nature of these shocks. In the past, major crises in developing countries usually had a regional concentration – as in the case of the East Asian financial crisis of 1997-98 or the Latin American tequila crisis of 1995. But the epicenter of the current crisis lies deep inside the developed economies, and therefore we would expect all developing regions to be damaged by the shocks. This simultaneity increases the risks of a serious global down turn.

The Global Picture

In summary, as these effects reinforce each other, there is a real risk that this global recession could be the most severe since the Great Depression of the 1930s. By the time it released its *World Economic Outlook* a few weeks ago, the IMF had already revised its projections for 2008 and 2009 downward by 0.2 and 0.9 per cent, respectively, since July. At 3.0 per cent, the projected growth of world output in 2009 is far below the 5.1 and 5.0 per cent growth achieved in 2006 and 2007 – even though China is projected to continue to grow strongly at a rate of over 9 per cent (International Monetary Fund 2008). At these rates, world output growth would drop back near levels last posted during the most recent global recession, in 2001-02. But the World Bank's upcoming forecasts are now projecting a global growth rate considerably lower still. And if the dramatic moves by the UK, Euro Zone countries, Japan, and US fail to revive lending, the recession will likely be much deeper than currently projected. This is especially true if gloomy consumer psychology leads to overshooting in asset markets on the way down, as it did on the way up.

CHAPTER

3

Islamic Finance

Search for a New World Order

The condition of third world developing countries under debt and inflation call for the search for a new world order with kind-hearted, after the exploitation of imperialistic powers with or without knowledge.

A large portion of world's wealth is vested in the hands of a rich minority. The results of the effort of the large number of debtors (people who takes loans from the banks) absorbing by the above minorities with the silent permission of the bankers, it is the passion of men for interest without a drop of sweat, through this money is kept under hoarding and do not possible the distribution for needed people, it is clearly an anti-social activity. The result is that , the need of money for trade and commerce is increased, the robbery of interest is emerged with the possibility of this situation. The traders can understand the after effects of the high interest loans through the failures of the new ventures. The hands of the entrepreneur is became empty after the payment of interest to the loan, because of this, decreased the capital investment in manufacturing sectors (worked with lack of people), decrease the production in factories, increase unemployment, and also decrease the purchasing power of the people.

In this situation the interest traders are detecting the decreasing demand of the money in the market, lack of the possibility they urged to decrease the interest rate. In this occasion the traders are depend the same money for loan. The crisis in world economy in a regular interval may happening because of the above reasons and it's side effects. The most tragic thing in this that, the ordinary people in the whole world always wandering with in the circle of this exploitation.

Each customer in a market always paid an indirect tax to the interest trader, the portion of interest rate of loan is paid by the trader with level of high price for the product, when the interest rate is high, the price of product also increased. In short the evils of the interest system is always suffered by the all ordinary people in the world.

The loans are received by the Government from the international banks for various projects, the duty for paying the interest is also in the shoulder of the citizen of the related country, statutory tax payment system is used by the government for transfer the burden to the people. Above are the simple picture of the evils of the interest system that created a hell in human life.

The search of men, for a permanent and suitable solution, that solving economic problems with a flexible and ever innovative designed economic law and procedures, the concept from the God is received as a alternative economics by the modern community because of it's popularity and philosophy.

What is Islamic Finance?

The Noble Qur'an is the basic source of Islam, presents Islam as a divine path of life which give guidance on all aspects of life, individual and social, political and economic, spiritual and temporal, national and international, and exhorts the Islamic community to work for the establishment of the socio-economic order of Islam, as according to the Holy Qur'an, it is the only way capable of achieving the welfare of man not only in this world but also in the hereafter.

The financial and economic principles of Islam are coming from the following sources.

- The Holy Qura'n.
- The Hadith (the traditions – the words and deeds of the prophet).
- Ijmah (consensus of the scholars).
- Quiyas (the analogy).

The first two elements are the most basic sources. The basic tenet of the Islamic economic system is the belief of *'Towheed'*. In the terminology of Islam this is known as the oneness of God. While the application of economic sphere, it means that God is the creator, sustainer, and hence the owner of everything, including all resources in the world. The Holy Qura'n states:

"To him belongs what is in the heavens, and earth, and all between them, and all beneath the soil" (20:6).

According to the Quranic verses God is the absolute owner of all resources, man, who is considered as the God's *'Khaleefa'* (vicegerent) on earth has been delegated only limited ownership rights. These rights are in the form of trusteeship rights. Being a trustee in regard to the resources, man is bound to manage the resources of the world in accordance with the whims and fancies of the real owner, God. This concept of ownership is the difference of Islamic economics and finance system from capitalism and socialism, as in the former individuals are absolute owners of resources and means of production and in the latter similar ownership rights are enjoyed by the state.

The second important precept of Islamic system is the faith in the Hereafter. Man's success in this life is to be judged not merely in terms of his gains in this life but more importantly in terms of his achievements in the Hereafter. Man has been instructed by Islam to give priority to the interests of Hereafter in case conflicts arise between compulsions of the here and those of the Hereafter. Its economic implication is that man should not take financial decision purely on the basis of pecuniary cost benefit considerations. Ethical consideration are equally or more important in financial decisions in the case of an Islamic man.

The ideological aim of Islam is the optimization of human welfare. Welfare here means not only the welfare of the present generation but also the future generation. With this in mind Islamic system envisages an economic order which ensures individual freedom, economic equity, and social justice.

Islamic financial principles are allows the private ownership of property as well as private enterprise. Simultaneously Islam also permits direct state intervention in economic activities. In application Islamic economic system is very similar to the modern mixed economies where both public and private sectors co-exist and co-function. Islamic economic system is run on financial as well moral incentives. Like capitalism, the major economic incentive in Islamic system is profit. Islam has permitted profit motive, although it has discouraged profiteering. Like socialist system Islam also institutes punishment with a view to ensuring the successful function of the economic order. Producers or investors who do not abide by the rules and restrictions to be observed in economic activities would be liable for punishment by the state here and by God Hereafter. This prevents a Muslim entrepreneur from investing in socially harmful products (for instance intoxicants or narcotics) or from resorting to exploitative practices (hoarding, profiteering).

The absence of interest is the unique distinguishing feature of an Islamic financial system. Prohibition of interest on the one hand cut at the root of the financial inequalities in the contemporary world and on the other increases the scope for profitable economic opportunities and the resultant increase in employment and income. The above result follow from the functional relationship existing between investment as well as interest rate and expected profitability, the theory is originally suggested by J. M. Keyens.

Definitions of Islamic Economics

Mohsin S. Khan, a senior economist at IMF says:

"Broadly speaking the term Islamic Economics' defines a complete system

Prescribes a specific pattern of social and economic behaviour for all individuals. It deals with a wide ranging set of issues, such as property rights, incentive system, allocation of resources, types of economic freedom, system of economic decision-making and proper role of the government. The over-riding objective of the system is social justice and specific patterns of income and wealth distribution and consequently economic policies are to be designed to achieve this ends".

S. M. Hasanuz Zaman, an IDB laureate in Islamic Economics, defined Islamic Economics:

"Islamic Economics is the Knowledge of application of injunctions and rules of the Shari'ah that stops injustice in the acquisition and disposition of material resources in order to provide satisfaction to individuals and enable them to perform their obligations to Allah and society".

Religious History of Islamic Economics

The Qurans's Economics:

"Those who consume interest shall not rise, except as he rises whom Satan by his touch prostrates [i.e. one who is misled]; 'Allah [God] has permitted trading but forbidden interest" [2:275].

Who so ever receives a warning from his/her Lord, he shall have his past gains, and his affair is committed to Allah; but who so ever reverts (to devouring interest) those, they are the inhabitants of the fire, therein dwelling forever". Clearly the Holy Qura'n, condemns the conventional, popular and profitable banking concept before it was actually put into wide scale practice. The standard bank generally participates as the intermediary between creditors and borrowers while making a profit on the margin at different interest rates. However, the 1970s proved that a new financial system was necessary to provide for religious exigencies within an economic framework. Islamic banking, or profit-loss-sharing (PLS), emerged as a response to conventional banking, creating an acceptable method that simultaneously satisfies financial needs and respects Islamic mandates.

An economic criticism of the conventional interest-based banking system portrays the dependency on interest as a useless instrument that contributes to the cyclical fluctuations in the economy. For instance, during the Great Depression as well as the recession of the 80s, interest rates were largely ineffective as a stabilisation tool. Former Secretary of State (US) Henry Kissinger stated, "The instability has persisted and the uncertainty has continued. After going through the throes of painfully high levels of inflation, the world economy has experienced a deep recession and unprecedented rate of unemployment, complicated further by high level of real interest rates and unhealthy exchange rate fluctuations".

With respect to religion, conventional banks did not provide an environment that acknowledged the restrictions expressed in Qura'n . The Qura'n, which is believed by the faithful to be the words of Allah that were revealed to his Prophet Muhammad, also contains Shari'ah laws that provide specific guidelines for economic and other secular endeavors. These laws emphasize five specific prohibitions that must be observed in order to establish a "just economic system free from all kinds of exploitation".

The Five Prohibitions in Financial Activities in Islam

Islamic economic law can be summarized into five specific bans and commandments.

1. Predetermined payment over and above the actual amount of principle is prohibited. This restriction is a ban on *riba*, or additional money, a concept that can be most closely translated to interest. The Qura'n further emphasizes that usury creates a group of capitalists where wealth is only circulated among a few hands in society.
2. Financiers should share in the profits and the losses. The Qura'n encourages investors to become partners as opposed to mere creditors. As a partner, each party is

significantly more involved with matters concerning how the money is spent. A partnership discourages unnecessary expenses on *haram* (unlawful) activities since both entities have a stake in the bottom line. In Islam a large emphasis is placed on the types of activities that an individual supports. However, by lending money the creditor has no say on how that money can be spent, and thus, could be supporting an activity that he/she is morally against. For these reasons the Qura'n encourages partnership investments where both parties can contribute to the activities that are taking place and similarly share in the profits and losses.

3. Making money from money is not acceptable. According to Islamic thought, money is not a commodity and must be viewed only as a medium of exchange with no intrinsic value. This core belief is what makes the interest, the collection or derivation of money on money, forbidden in Islam.
4. *Gharar,* considerable uncertainty or risk, is prohibited. Islam discourages transactions, such as options, futures, and foreign exchange rates, in which both parties do not have perfect knowledge regarding the values intended to be exchanged. Such transactions without perfect knowledge are considered to be speculative in nature.
5. The final law states that all economic transactions should support those practices or products which are not considered *haram*, or unlawful, to Islam. This distinction goes beyond the idea of interest, encompassing the exclusion of investments in areas such as alcohol, casinos, and cigarettes.

The Important Principles of Islamic Finance

The Principle of Tawheed and Brotherhood

Islamic economics is not content with the conventional viewpoint of economic analysis. It is motivated by its first cardinal principal – the principle of 'Tawheed' and Brotherhood. 'Tawheed' literally means unit. In the economic context it summarizes the crux of the entire essence of Islamic economics in that it teaches man how to relate and deal with other men in the light of his relationship with God. It says that behind the workings of an economy based on market exchange, the allocation of resources, the maximization of utility and profits, is a more fundamental truth – that of social justice. In Islam the capacity to understand and dispense this social justice emanates from the knowledge and practice of the principles of the Quran. In this way the principle of Tawheed and Brotherhood links up our duties to men with our duties to God. In more practical terms the essence of Tawheed and Brotherhood lies in equality and cooperation. The Quran verily says, 'O mankind! be mindful of your duties to your Lord who created you from a single soul and from it created its mate and from them twain has spread abroad a multitude of men and women.

An immediate corollary of the principle of Tawheed and Brotherhood is the predominant note of Islamic economics, that to God alone belongs whatever is in the heavens and in the earth, and that He has made the good things for the service of man 3. Man has been created as the vicegerent of God on earth entrusted with the just use and distribution of His resources.

The Principle of Work and Productivity

The second basic principle of Islamic economics is that of work and compensation for work performed. It states that an individual's wages must be proportionate to the amount and category of labour performed by him. The amount of labour would be measured in, say, man-hours of work and the category of labour would be specific to different professions. The wages in the latter case would be constrained by the minimum of the rent determined for the category of labour in demand.

Whenever an individual acquires income greater than what is due to him by dint of his input of labour and other resources, which produce this income, he commits what is known as 'rububiyyah', that is, sole proprietorship of the means of production. Because Islamic economic ideas hold that fundamentally all means of production belong to God, so an individual by transgressing this limit commits a form of excess.

Under this category of excess are included rent on land and sharecropping, but rent on money capital is permitted. As regards the prohibition of the rent on plain land we have the hadith (saying) of Prophet Muhammad, that 'He who has a land should cultivate it and should not rent it – not even for a third or fourth of its crop and not for a specific amount of food'. Inherent in this hadith is the problem of value. Uncultivated land has not received the labour of the owner and is therefore, not liable to a price until it is exploited to produce. Thus, in the first case we have the idea of value in use and in the second case the idea of value in exchange.

It must be noted that rent was prohibited only on plain land, and not on land in which there has been input of labour and capital by the owner. In the latter case it would be an act of injustice towards the landowner to have him forego for nothing in return, the exchange value created in the land by his labour and capital inputs. However, it is suggested strongly that this rent cannot be in crops, but in money terms. In this regard we have the following tradition mentioned by Abu Dawud, who quoted Sa'd Ibn Waqqas, a compansion of Prophet Muhammad, as saying, 'We used to rent land and pay the owner as rent the produce on the banks of the irrigation canals. The Prophet prohibited this and ordered us to pay rent in gold and silver'. Thus, while rent was prohibited on plain land, it was allowed in cultivated and used land. Sharecropping was prohibited..

The Principle of Distributional Equity

The third major principle of Islamic economics is the right of society to redistribute private property. This is amply supported in several Quranic verses.8 The chief items of national income and transfer payments used for redistributive purposes in an Islamic economy are zakah (tax on wealth exceeding a certain exemption level called nisab), sadaqah (voluntary charity), ghanimah (war booty), fai (property acquired in war without fighting), fidth (a part offai whose distribution pattern is similar to zakah), kharaj (tax on lands conquered during war), 'ushr (zakah on crops).

There is no order in the Quran that the various sources of funds must be spent in strict accordance with the practice during the early period of Islam. It is just the broad principles of expenditure of these funds as laid down in the Quran and further elaborated through the Islamic legal sources, such as the hadith (traditions of Prophet Muhammad), fiqh (legal study based on original sources) and shariah (Islamic law as it pertains to different affairs of life), that must remain invariant. For example, the way the four-fifths of ghanimah was distributed among the Muslim soldiers in the early period of Islam was only an exigency at a time when wars were thrust on the Muslims before an Islamic state could be established. In these conditions there existed no standing army nor a state treasury to finance a standing army. Therefore, the Muslim soldiers during that early formative period were allowed their share of the war acquisitions. However, in a modern Islamic state the army could be regularly paid as are civil servants and war acquisitions would be added to the state treasury.

Similarly, the remaining one-fifth of ghanimah can go to the state treasury to supplement organized forms of social assistance programmes. The part due to the Prophet and his near kin during the early period of Islam can now be returned to the government for public works.

Similar is the case with zakah expenditure in the form of an organized social assistance programme undertaken by the state. The stated categories of expenditure of the zakah fund can be extended to cover programmes of employment creation, family welfare, rehabilitation of the aged, unemployment insurance, income support during times of economic losses and others. Even the rate of zakah, originally fixed at 2.5 per cent on all forms of assessed wealth exceeding nisab level at any given point of time can be varied but only marginally.

At the more micro-level the Islamic law of inheritance helps to redistribute private property. The Quran is clear on this point. 'The primary motive of the law of inheritance is to put a final check on the concentration of material assets in the hands of a few.

In short therefore, equitable redistribution of income and wealth is incumbent upon the Islamic state and the individual, and has to take place fundamentally on the basis of Tawheed and Brotherhood. The objective of this redistribution is to increase the productive transformation of national income and wealth to the employment and welfare of the citizens. Thus, when the early Muslim refugees, evicted from Mecca found refuge in the city of Medina, they became members of that society and were treated on equal terms and not confined to camps and charities. If a refugee could cultivate land he was given land to do so; if he had traits of a trader, he was allowed to open a business; whoever could not manage, had the help of a brother in faith.

Interest Free Element in Islamic Finance

It is useful to begin examining the Islamic Financing system by first defining some basic terminology. Riba is the Arabic word for the predetermined return on the use of money. In the past there has been dispute about whether Riba refers to interest or usury, but there is now consensus among Muslim scholars that the term covers all forms of interest, and not only 'excessive' interest. Thus, in the ensuing discussion the terms Riba and 'interest' will be used interchangeably, and an Islamic banking system will be one in which the payment or receipt of interest is forbidden. An interest-based, or traditional, banking system is defined as symmetrical, with interest being paid and charged for the use of funds.

The Islamic restriction against interest is quite explicit and has to be taken as axiomatic. Transactions based on Riba are strictly prohibited in the Quran, as the following verse forcefully states:

Those who devour Riba will not stand except as stands one whom the devil hath driven to madness by [his] touch. (11:275)

To see that there can be no doubt of the condemnation of the system of interest, and the penalties that would be imposed if the rule were not observed, consider the following verse:

"O ye who believe! Observe your duty to Allah and give up what remains [due to you] from Riba, if ye are [in truth] believers. And if ye do not, then be warned of war [against you] from Allah and His Messenger. And if ye repent then ye have your principal [without Riba]. Wrong not, and ye shall not be wronged". (11:278-79)

Although there have been discussions among Muslim scholars on the reasons for this prohibition against interest, it is obvious from the above quotations that there is no real room for differences in interpretation about whether interest can or cannot be paid in an Islamic economy. It is the general view that it is considerations of equity and protection of the poor that lie behind the strong condemnation of interest-based transactions. In any case, the Islamic economic system, and of course the corresponding banking system, has to operate within the prescribed framework, which does not permit interest.

The concept of an economy in which interest is not allowed appears quite counterintuitive to many observers. Arguments that such a system is unlikely to work efficiently in the short run, and in the long run will result in an eventual drying up of savings and investment, have frequently been made in this connection. This view, however, tends to reflect a basic confusion between the terms 'rate of interest' and 'rate of return'. Whereas Islam clearly forbids the former, it not only permits, but rather encourages, trade and therefore profits. For example, consider this verse from the Quran:

"That is, because they say: Trade is just like Riba; whereas Allah permitteth trading and forbiddeth Riba". (11:275)

Intangible rewards are also permitted; using the Arabic term Sadaqat, for charity or alms, the next verse from the Quran says that:

"Allah has blighteth Riba and made Sadaqat fruitful". (11:276).

In essence, what is forbidden in Islam is the fixed or pre-determined return on financial transactions and not an uncertain rate of return, such as that represented by profits. From this distinction it follows that, if a banking structure could evolve in which the return for the use of money would fluctuate according to actual profits made from such use, the resultant system would be consistent with the guidelines of Islam.

The hostility to interest is based on the belief that the Qur'an bans all interest, regardless of its rate or form. In fact, what the Qur'an bans is riba, the pre-Islamic Arabian practice of doubling the debt of a borrower unable to make restitution on schedule, including both the principal and the accumulated interest. Riba tended to push defaulters into enslavement, so it was an acute source of social friction. From the earliest days of Islam to the present, various interpreters of the Qur'an have held, accordingly, that the purpose of the ban on riba was simply to block socially harmful financial practices. In particular, they have suggested that the ban was intended, like the bankruptcy laws of a modem state, to make creditors deal charitably with debtors unable to make timely payment.

Nevertheless, for the past half-century, opposition to interest has been treated as the *sine qua non* of being an 'Islamic' economist. To be recognised as an Islamic economist, it is not sufficient to be a learned Muslim who contributes to economic debates. One must be opposed in principle to all interest, including not only the monopolistic returns of rural moneylenders in financially underdeveloped countries, but also the competitive returns of commercial banks in the industrialised world. Thus, the focus of Islamic economics is neither on ways to keep interest rates within bounds nor on keeping financial markets competitive. Rather, it is on the eradication of interest.

There exists no example, ancient or modern, of a country that has done away with interest. Although there have always been groups hostile to interest – especially in economically primitive communities in no large community have interest-based financial deals ever become uncommon. Islamic economists have made great efforts, therefore, to justify a ban in terms that go beyond the simple claim that the Qur'an demands it. A common argument, found in all popular texts on Islamic economics is that it is unjust to earn money without assuming risk. By the logic of this argument, it is unjust for a bank to earn interest on an industrial loan, for the arrangement places the risk of the financed venture entirely on the industrialist, allowing the bank to earn a return even if the venture fails. Likewise, it is unjust for a saver to earn interest on her savings deposits; the investments financed through her savings could go sour, in which case her bank would lose money while she, the deposit holder, still earns the predetermined return. Whatever the merits of the notion of risk-free returns, the crux of the argument is that profit is legitimate only as a reward for risk. Accordingly, banking must be based on the sharing of both risk and profit, which rules out interest. It is permissible, of course, for an individual to put money in a bank for safekeeping, provided no interest payments are involved.

The literature on Islamic banking does not specify how a depositor and his bank, or the bank and a borrower, are to apportion risk. It insists only that each of the parties to a financial contract must bear some share of the risk. In principle, one side could carry just one-twentieth of the risk, although some writers caution that the risk shares must conform to customary notions of fairness. Always left unclear is why it would be unjust for one side to accept most, or even all, of the risk if, as is commonly the case, the parties differ in their capacity to bear risk. Consider a bank and one of its 50,000 depositors, a retired widow whose sole source of income is what she earns on her modest savings. The widow is likely to be averse to putting her capital at risk, for a sufficiently large loss would leave her destitute. By contrast, the bank may easily pay her a fixed return, and thus bear the full risk of investing her savings, for it is able to minimize its overall exposure to risk through diversification.

In any modern economy, one will find bank depositors who are happy to put their capital at risk for the promise of a greater return. Also, one will find banks that are willing to earn a variable return on some, even all, of their assets in order to raise their expected earnings. So where financial intermediaries are free to choose their preferred mixes of fixed and variable earnings, and likewise for their lending commitments, competitive pressures will provide economic agents who are averse to interest opportunities to participate in deals of the kind Islamic economists characterize as 'profit and loss sharing'.

The relative popularity of profit and loss sharing arrangements will depend on factors such as informational asymmetries between the providers and users of funds, the costs of managing variable-commitment contracts, and the efficiency of the legal system-in addition, of course, to the pattern of risk preferences.

In an unregulated economy, then, nothing would block the emergence of banks that Islamic economics defines as 'Islamic'. And if banking based on profit and loss sharing is in practice not as common as one might want or expect, the reason is likely to be that the contracting options available to financial intermediaries are restricted-as they are in, for instance, the United States, where banking regulations have long limited the risks banks may accept on their investments and those they may impose on their depositors. Yet, what the Islamic economists demand is not just financial deregulation aimed at generating more profit and loss sharing. They desire to replace existing regulations with new regulations that would force all banks to limit themselves to variable earnings and commitments. The reason, once again, is that they interpret the ban on riba as a condemnation of all fixed financial instruments. And they want interest-based banking outlawed, on the grounds that the recipients of interest income achieve gains without assuming any risk what so ever.

This justification rests, as Abul Halim Ismail (paper presented in IIUM-1990) notes, on a serious misunderstanding concerning the sources of financial risk. Contrary to the perceptions of Islamic economists, a bank that earns interest on its assets is not engaged in risk-free business. It might fail to collect on some of its loans; an unanticipated economic slump might leave it with too large a workforce; and it is always possible that, after the terms of a long-term loan have been set, macroeconomic conditions will force it to raise the returns it offers depositors, thus reducing its profitability. Similarly, an interest-earning depositor carries some risk, if only because his bank may fail. It is true, of course, that as a practical matter, deposit insurance will eliminate the depositor's risk, but most Islamic economists reject such insurance as un-Islamic. In the view that the existing economic systems suffer from too much risk avoidance, they wish to expose individuals to more risk-precisely the opposite of what deposit insurance seeks to achieve.

A system that asks economic agents to assume risks they would rather avoid is unlikely to perform as planned. In fact, the Islamic banks have been operating very differently from the idealised financial intermediaries described in textbooks on Islamic Economics.

Development and Present Condition

The Growth

The popularity of this form of financing has gained momentum in the Muslim world as it grows at a rate of 15 per cent per annum. Thus far, Islamic banks have managed to muster over $200 billion worth of *Shari'ah*-compliant assets in over 75 countries.

Twenty years ago Muslims seeking to engage in financial products while still honoring their religious beliefs faced very limited options. However, the financial accommodations mentioned above clearly prove that Islamic Banking has emerged as one of the fastest growing sectors of finance in the world. Yet, the impressive growth of Islamic banking is neither due to increased awareness of Islam nor an expanding population of Muslims. Rather, over the last 15-20 years a significant number of devout Muslims, especially in the Middle East, have accumulated a large volume of wealth. The accumulation of all this wealth resulted in the development of financial institutions providing these depositors with roughly comparable returns and religiously acceptable banking activities.

Atif Abdulmalik, CEO of Bahrain's First Islamic Bank, claims that the transfer of wealth from the state to private individuals in the Arabian Gulf will be a driving force for Islamic financing. "Money in private hands fuels Islamic banking because people go to hell and governments don't". As competition continues to grow, financial products within Islamic banking will begin to develop similar characteristics and risk/return profiles to their more traditional counterparts. This evolution would result in a huge transfer of assets from the conventional bank to the Islamic bank, as Muslim investors would choose the Islamically acceptable investment over a standard product that yields the same return.

In Bahrain, Malaysia, and even the U.K., the demand for Islamic financing is growing and several industry leaders including HSBC and Citibank have already developed Islamic Banking operations. Currently, 8 per cent of Malaysia's banking sector is based on Islamic principles and is expected to increase to 20 per cent by 2010. The Kuala Lumpur Stock Exchange "has its own syariah [*Shari'ah*] index to monitor the performance of listed *halal* counters [Islamically acceptable securities]".

Impact on Western Financial Markets

Twenty years ago investors who wanted to invest under *Shari-ah* had only the option of earning zero per cent interest. However, today with the creation of these various Islamic investment alternatives, Muslim investors are no longer at such a severe disadvantage. There are currently 106 Islamic mutual funds globally, totaling well over $3 billion in assets. These funds are *Shari'ah* compliant and follow strict guidelines as to the companies in which they invest. Perhaps, one of the most significant indications of acceptance into the western financial system is the development of benchmarks for Islamically viable equities. The London and New York Stock Exchanges, the two most advanced equity exchanges in the world, now have a point of reference for which Muslims can compare the performance of their *Shari'ah*-compliant investments: The FTSE Global Islamic Index (London Stock Exchange) and the Dow Jones Islamic Market Index (NYSE). The Dow Jones currently has 9 Islamic market indices, tracking investments in other countries and regions as well as an Islamic Market Technology Index. The methodology used by the Dow Jones in selecting securities within these indices is as follows:

- Exclude all companies in the following industries: alcohol, tobacco, pork-related products, financial services, defense/weapons, entertainment (hotels, casinos, gambling, cinema, pornography, and music).
- Exclude companies if Total Debt divided by Trailing 12-Month Average Market Capitalization is greater than or equal to 33 per cent.
- Exclude companies if the sum of Cash and Interest Bearing Securities divided by Trailing 12-Month Average Market Capitalization is greater than or equal to 33 per cent.
- Exclude companies if Accounts Receivables divided by Total Assets is greater than or equal to 45.

Since these Islamic benchmarks restrict stock selection to a limited set of industries, a concern exists that they might not accurately reflect the general equity markets; thus, impedes Muslim investors from a comparable standpoint to evaluate their investment performance. A data analysis conducted against the U.S., equity market confirms the accuracy of the Dow Jones Islamic U.S. Market Index (IMUS). Considering that the IMUS tracks 621 *Shari'ah* compliant stocks, the S and P proves to be a valid benchmark with a portfolio that follows 500 companies. Exhibit 1 compares the index prices from May 1999 to October 2002 as well as their per cent returns (only available information for IMUS). The similarity in the standard deviations of the returns (.0529 for S&P and .0593 for IMUS) and the correlation between the two index prices of 95.3 per cent confirm that little difference exists in the risk profiles of the irrespective domains. Therefore, the research suggests Muslim investors should be able to obtain similar performance levels on their investments in U.S., equity markets.

The Profit and Loss Sharing Principle (PLSP)

The PLSP is related to the *Musharaka* principle in Islamic Finance. Profits are distributed according to contrctually agreed shares, but the liability of loss is proportionate to the capital contribution. The priciple was first mentioned by Anwar Iqbal Qurishi (*Islam and the theory of interest-1947*) but formally discussed by S. Mahmud Ahmad (*Economics of Islam-1947*). According to Ahmad, may take one of two forms: shares may be floated by ordinary joint stock companies in accordance with the *Musharaka* principle, or banking institutions may mobilize resources on the basis of *Mudaraba* principle.

Among muslim economists Umar Chapra (*towards a just monetary system-1985*) assigns an important role to the Mushrakah principle for two important reasons . First he does not present any model of atypical financial intermediation system as do M.N.Siddiqi. *Second*, his emphasis is on institutional arrangements which characterisze the Islamic financing institutions more as investment institutions than as typical financial intermediaries. The natural outcome of such arrangements is expected to provide a much more fertile ground for *Musharaka*. On the other hand due to its nature, the two-tier-*Mudaraba* was suitable as a basis of the intermediation system.

CHAPTER

How Islamic Finance as a Solution for Global Financial Crisis

Throughout the current economic and financial crisis one contrarian statistic has stood out. Financial assets offered by the Islamic Financial Services Industry (IFSI) and generally classified as *'Shariah-compliant'*, were less affected by the crisis. Italian Economist Loretta Napoleoni during a seminar at the University of New Mexico proclaimed, *"Islamic finance... [a] system [that] could help us to get out of the current crisis"*. Writing in the influential Turkish daily-*Today's Zaman*, famous Turkish columnist Ibrahim Ozturk declared, *"Islamic finance has entered a bright new stage of development, emerging after the global financial crisis as a more equitable and efficient alternative to the Western approach"*. The widely read Arabic daily-*Asharq Al Awsat* [Saudi-London] opined, *"Islamic banks are untouched by the current crisis due to the nature of Islamic banking especially that it does not deal in debt trading and distances itself from market speculation that takes place in European and American banks"*. How do such claims stack up against reality? Is Islamic finance different enough from conventional finance to avoid its pitfalls?

The IFSI, which has marketed itself as being an alternative to the conventional financial system, has come a long way from its rather modest and relatively recent beginnings. The IFSI was recently estimated by Moody's to be worth $700 billion and projected by the Islamic Development Bank to be $2.8 trillion by 2015. By 2015, majority of the IFSI will be geographically centered in the Gulf Co-operation Council (GCC) region while the South Asian region will provide about 15 to 25 per cent of the total services. The IFSI encompasses almost all of the institutional and architectural features of the conventional finance industry. However, it should be noted that the size of IFSI relative to the Conventional Finance Industry (CFI) is very small (about 2%). In other words the IFSI has not been sufficiently stress tested to proclaim its efficacy when applied to a broader set of economic situations.

One distinguishing feature of IFSI has been its insistence that in complying with Shariah (the jurisprudence of Islam) it considers dealing with interest as totally unacceptable. The avoidance of interest reflects verses in the Holy Quran (3:130; 2:175; 4:161) which forbid riba, most often and commonly translated as interest rates. The IFSI contends that it has replaced interest rates with rate of profit on equity, profit sharing finance and markup transactions.

In practice, the contracts of the IFSI fall short of the 'interest-free' claims it makes. IFSI contracts do allow for presence of interest rates, mostly indirectly but sometimes directly, even though in small measures. Islamic mutual funds for example allow investment in stocks of companies that use interest based debt (current practices allow 33% debt-ratios). Sukuks, described as Islamic bonds, guarantee a fixed rate of return, which to most financial observers look like interest. In murabaha, Islamic jurists opine that home buyer (mortgagor) is involved in credit sales and not a loan contract (as in traditional mortgages). Yet murabaha loan documents use the conventional terms like 'note', 'loan', and 'interest' to describe its features much like any home mortgage contract. Moreover, the mark-up used in murabaha is usually benchmarked to a conventional interest rate.

This has given rise to what Rice University's Mahmoud El-Gamal critically calls *Shariah*-arbitrage, defined as the practice of extracting premium rents from participants in a captive-market for products labeled and perceived to be *Shariah* compliant. The paradox is not merely of academic interest. Among the producers and users of Islamic financial products there is pervasive skepticism. A unique insight about this perception is gathered from a recent research on the attitude of customers and bankers using IFSI. A significant majority (6 in 10) believe that the development of Islamic banking has more to do with being faithful to Islam than any other criterion (although the proponents of Islamic finance often cite the superiority of IFSI is due to its purported commitment to social justice and welfare). Nearly 7 in 10 believe that the 'rate of profit' or 'markup profit' charged by Islamic banks do not differ much from interest based transactions offered by the CFI. Potential patrons (7 in 10) are unwilling to transact with the IFSI because they do not find much difference between the IFSI and the CFI.

In discussing how bankruptcy courts are likely to rule on foreclosures under IFSI contracts like *ijarah* (lease-based transactions), *murabaha* (cost plus markup sale) and *musharaka* (partnership contract), legal experts observe, "We would not anticipate that this type of foreclosure would differ materially from that of a conventional mortgage foreclosure.... The 'borrower' holds all the benefits and risks of ownership in a *Musharaka* transaction as well". As such in bankruptcy and foreclosure proceedings, IFSI providers have the same legal protections as those afforded to CFI institutions in debt based transactions.

The current state of IFSI is prohibition driven primarily centered on taking existing CFI contracts and pronouncing the Islamicity or lack thereof for those contracts. The IFSI then proceeds to institute contractual changes that alter the structure of the contract to make them contractually *Shariah-compliant* without addressing any of their possibly inherent fault lines. This process is enabled by Shariah-boards, which pronounce the Islamicity of such contracts. The *Shariah*-boards are beset with agency problems (conflict of interest) as they are not subjected to disclosure rules equivalent in scale and scope to those for corporate boards, which many argue are in urgent need for more reform and transparency themselves! According to a recent study the top 5 *Shariah*-scholars makeup 15 per cent of the entire universe of *Shariah* board positions. Only 180 scholars are involved in nearly 1000 *Shariah* board positions. This stifles innovations and fosters unhealthy imitations.

One thing is clear, if Islamic Finance is to remain restricted to Muslims then not only will Islamic Finance not save the day but it will also pervert the mission of Prophet Muhammad, described in the Quran (21:07) as a mercy to all humanity (creation, to be precise). The emphasis on the prohibition based aspects of Shariah have led to missed opportunities to promote them aqasid or objectives of Shariah whose aims are not prohibition-driven but rather, inclusive and egalitarian. The *maqasid* or objectives of *Shariah*, is to protect and preserve life, mind, faith, property and offspring, which according to the noted Andalusian Islamic scholar Abu Ishaq al-Shatibi is a set of objectives that are common to all religions and must be the transcendent framework to evaluate all Islamic law, social obligations and contracts (financial or otherwise). The attainment of these goals require the development of a positive and inclusive vision, which can truly address the many shortcomings that plagues the world of finance – from bad regulation, to un-transparent contracts, to plain old greed.

Islamic finance has a role to play in the world of finance. But to do so, the IFSI will have to de-emphasize its innovations based on *Shariah*-arbitrage and engage in developing a more holistic vision that will resonate with all people of conscience, not just Muslims. Islamic mutual funds, for instance, will have to beyond the negative screens it primarily imposes in selecting stocks to developing positive screens that steer investments towards those opportunities that can lead to sustainable development strategies. Islamic finance must also promote the highest ethical standards and the most transparent disclosure rules, enabling a healthy dose of sunshine into the complex world of financial engineering (responsible for the now infamous credit default swaps that produced the toxic home loans). Islamic banks must also provide a positive vision of efficient and effective distribution of zakat wealth. Islamic financial institutions must develop innovative programmes to produce equity based partnerships with small and medium enterprises, which are often the forgotten sector in the world of high finance. The Islamic financial service industry can truly differentiate itself by adopting a more socially conscious role that will enable them to not only fulfill the objectives of *Shariah* but also inject an alternative vision into the world of global finance allowing a necessary paradigm shift if only to avoid another global economic crisis.

Primary Cause of the Crises

There are undoubtedly a number of causes. The generally recognised most important cause is, however, excessive and imprudent lending by banks. One cannot blame banks for this because, like everyone else, they also wish to maximize their profits in a materialist cultural environment where maximization of income and wealth is the highest measure of human achievement. The more credit they extend, the higher will be their profit. It is high leverage which enables excessive lending. Excessive lending, however, leads to an unsustainable boom in asset prices followed by an artificial rise in consumption and speculative investment. The higher the leverage the more difficult it is to unwind it in a down turn. Unwinding gives rise to a vicious cycle of selling that feeds on itself and leads to a steep decline in asset prices followed by a serious financial crisis, particularly if it is also accompanied by over indulgence in short sales.

It is the combined influence of three forces which can help prevent the recurrence of crises. One of these is moral constraints on the greed to maximize profit, wealth and consumption by any means in keeping with the mores of the prevailing secular and materialist culture. The second is market discipline which is expected to exercise a restraint on leverage, excessive lending and derivatives. The third is reform of the system's structure along with prudential regulation and supervision appropriately designed to prevent crises, achieve sustainable development and safeguard social interest. Since all of these three forces have become blunted by the philosophies of secularism, materialism and liberalism, mankind has been flooded with different man-made problems, including recurring financial crises, family disintegration, flagrant inequalities of income and wealth, and crime and anomie.

This raises the question of why market discipline has not been able to exercise a restraint on excessive lending. Is it possible that market discipline is not adequate in the financial system? If this is the case, then why is it so? The market can impose a discipline primarily through incentives and deterrents. If incentives and deterrents do not exist or become weak, market discipline will also become weak.

The incentives and deterrents come through the prospect of making profit or loss. The major source of profit in the conventional system is the interest that the banks earn through their lending operations. The loss comes through the inability to recover these loans with interest. One would, therefore, expect that banks would carefully analyze their lending operations so as not to undertake those that would lead to a loss. There would be a check over excessive lending if the banks were afraid of suffering losses that would reduce their net profit. This does not happen in a system where profit and loss sharing (PLS) does not exist, and the repayment of loans with interest is generally guaranteed.

There are two factors that enable banks to assume that they will not suffer losses. The first of these is the collateral, which is indispensable and unavoidable in any financial system for managing the risk of default. The collateral can, of course, do this only if it is of good quality. Collateral is, however, exposed to a valuation risk. Its value can be impaired by the same factors that diminish the borrowers ability to repay. The collateral, cannot, therefore, be a substitute for a more careful evaluation of the project financed. However, if there is no risk-sharing, the banks may not always undertake a careful evaluation of the collateral and extend financing for any purpose, including speculation. This may be more so if it is possible for banks to transfer the risk of default by selling the debt to someone else. The second factor that provides protection to the banks is the 'too big to fail' concept which assures them that the central bank will bail them out. (See Miskhin, 1997, p. 61). Banks which are provided with such a safety net have incentives to take greater risks than what they otherwise would (Mishkin, 1997, p. 62).

Given that banks lend excessively to maximize their profit, why is it that the depositors do not impose a discipline on the banks? They can do so in several different ways: by demanding better management, greater transparency, and more efficient risk management. If this does not work, they can always punish the banks by withdrawing their deposits. They do not, however, do so in the conventional financial system because they are assured of the repayment of their deposits with interest. (Mishkin, 1997, p. 62). This makes them complacent and they do not take as much interest in the affairs of their financial institution as they would if they expected to suffer losses.

The false sense of immunity from losses provided to bankers as well as depositors impairs the ability of the market to impose the required discipline. This leads to an unhealthy expansion in the overall volume of credit, to excessive leverage, to even subprime debt, and to living beyond means. This tendency of the system gets further reinforced by the bias of the tax system in favour of debt financing – dividends are subject to taxation while interest payments are allowed to be treated as a tax-deductible expense.

This shows that the absence of risk/reward sharing reduces market discipline and, thereby, introduces a fault line in the financial system. It is this fault line that makes it possible for the financier to lend excessively and also to move funds rapidly from place to place at the slightest change in the economic environment. A high degree of volatility thus gets injected into interest rates and asset prices. This generates uncertainty in the investment market, which in turn discourages capital formation and leads to misallocation of resources. (BIS, 1982, p. 3). It also drives the borrowers and lenders alike from the long end of the debt market to the shorter end. Consequently, there is a steep rise in highly leveraged short-term debt, which has accentuated economic and financial instability. The IMF acknowledged this fact in its May 1998 *World Economic Outlook* by stating that countries with high levels of short-term debt are "likely to be particularly vulnerable to internal and external shocks and thus susceptible to financial crises" (p. 83).

One may wish to pause here to ask why a rise in debt, and particularly short-term debt, should accentuate instability? One of the major reasons for this is the close link between easy availability of credit, macroeconomic imbalances, and financial instability. The easy availability of credit makes it possible for the public sector to have high debt profile and for the private sector to live beyond its means and to have high leverage. If the debt is not used productively, the ability to service the debt does not rise in proportion to the debt and leads to financial fragility and debt crises. The greater the reliance on short-term debt and the higher the leverage, the more severe the crises may be. This is because short-term debt is easily reversible as far as the lender is concerned, but repayment is difficult for the borrower if the amount is locked up in loss-making speculative assets or medium – and long-term investments with a long gestation period.

While there may be nothing basically wrong in a reasonable amount of short-term debt that is used for financing the purchase and sale of real goods and services by households, firms, and governments, an excess of it tends to get diverted to unproductive uses as well as speculation in the foreign exchange, stock, and property markets. Jean Claude Trichet, President of the European Central Bank, has rightly pointed out that "a bubble is more likely to develop when investors can leverage their positions by investing borrowed funds" (Trichet, 2005, p. 4).

If we examine some of the major crises in the international financial system like the one in East Asia, the instability in the foreign exchange markets, collapse of the Long-term Capital Management (LTCM) hedge fund, and the prevailing crisis in the U.S., financial system, we find that the easy availability of credit and the resultant steep rise in debt, particularly short-term debt, are the result of inadequate market discipline in the financial markets due to the absence of risk sharing. (Chapra, 2007, pp. 166-173). In this paper I will refer only to the collapse of the LTCM, the prevailing imbalances in the US economy, and the subprime mortgage crisis in the US financial system.

The Collapse of Long-term Capital Management

The collapse of the U.S., hedge fund LTCM in 1998 was due to highly leveraged short-term lending. Even though the name hedge fund brings to mind the idea of risk reduction, "hedge funds typically do just the opposite of what their name implies: they speculate" (Edwards 1999, p. 189). They are "nothing more than rapacious speculators, borrowing heavily to beef up their bets" (*The Economist* 1998, p. 21). These hedge funds are mostly unregulated and are not encumbered by restrictions on leverage or short sales and are free to take concentrated positions in a single firm, industry, or sector – positions that might be considered 'imprudent' if taken by other institutional fund managers (Edwards, 1999, p. 190; Sulz, 2007, p. 175) They are, therefore, able to pursue the investment or trading strategies they choose in their own interest without due regard to the impact that this may have on others. They now account for close to half the trading on the New York and London stock exchanges (Sulz, 2007, p. 175).

The Prevailing Imbalances in the U.S. Economy

The lack of discipline in the financial system has also created two serious problems for the United States. Both of these, the public-sector budgetary deficits and the private-sector saving deficiency, ring a worrisome note not only for the United States but also for the world economy. The federal government has been running budgetary deficits ever since 1970, except for a brief respite between 1998 and 2001. The budget moved from a surplus of $255 billion in fiscal year 2000 to a deficit of $412 billion in 2004 (Kohn, 2005, pp. 1-2; and IMF, August 2008, p. 602). The deficit declined thereafter to $317, $248 billion and $163 billion in 2005, 2006 and 2007. (IMF, August 2008, p. 1188), but is estimated to have risen to a record $438 billion in fiscal 2008. Instead of declining, the deficits are expected to rise further in the near future as the government tries to stabilize the financial system by buying illiquid assets from financial institutions, fulfils campaign pledges, and the baby boomers reach retirement age.

The Subprime Mortgage Crisis

The subprime mortgage crisis in the grip of which the US finds itself at present is also a reflection of excessive lending. Securitisation or the 'originate-to distribute' model of financing has played a crucial role in this. There is no doubt that securitisation was a useful innovation. It provided lenders greater access to capital markets, lowered transactions costs, and allowed risks to be shared more widely. The resulting increase in the supply of mortgage credit contributed to a rise in the home ownership rate from 64 per cent in 1994 to 68 per cent in 2007 (Bernanke, 20 September 2007, p. 1).

Justification for Islamic Financial System-Under Economic Crisis

1. *Efficiency of Islamic Financial System*

Islamic financial system avoids the use of interest based lending in macroeconomic level. The rate of profit on equity and profit sharing finance is applied against the rate of interest, and by markups on credit-purchase finance and by rental rates on leasing finance. While the time-value of money is maintained, there is no need to handle the complicated questions of how to bring the rate of interest down to zero in order to reach the optimal allocation of resources.

The conventional financial system allocates financial resources with supreme regard for borrower's ability to repay the principal amount and interest. Islamic financial system is based on equity and profit sharing, aim would be on the profitability and rate of the concerned investment. This system of finance helps to lead the resources to the most productive investments. This would increase efficiency of the financing process and reinforce the efficiency in the real sectors.

The Islamic Financial System is based on the mark-up finance the acquisition of goods and services, including productive assets. The cost of the finance, or mark-up, will depend on the relative value in use of each commodity, when an open market with sufficient competition, whether in consumption or production. Optimum resource allocation is again possible.

2. *Stability in Islamic Financial System*

In the conventional banking system follows the one hand liabilities that include demand time and saving deposits, which the bank guarantees. Mostly debt instruments are include as asset in the bank, the quality of the instruments depends on the ability of the corresponding debtor to repay. The defaults of the asset side create a dilemma to meet the predetermined obligations of the bank, such defaults will be happening at the time of crisis. Only demand deposits are guaranteed in an Islamic Bank, it has the liabilities of different nature.

CHAPTER

5

Islamic Law of Contracts

Islamic commercial law, known as fiqh muammalat in Islamic legal term, constitutes an important branch of law dealing with issues of contracts and the legal effect(s) arising from a contract; be it a valid, void or avoidable contract respectively. Contract is Islamic law, on the other hand is a complex legal discipline in both its jurisprudential foundation and its practical function. Also contract covers a variety of dealings and transactions to meet the needs of the society. No doubt, issues of commercial transactions, unlike devotional issues ('ibadat), are ever lasting and bound to change due to the changing circumstances and situations of both the object and subject of the transactions. Therefore it is not surprising that the first article of the *Majallah al-Ahkam al-'Adliyyah* (the civil code of the Ottoman Empire) endorses the idea that man is social by nature and that social life is essential to him, stating that, "in view of the fact that man is social by nature, he cannot live in solitude like other animals, but is need of co-operation with his fellow men in order to promote an urban society. Every person, however, seeks the things which suit him and is vexed by any competition. As a result, it has been necessary to establish laws to maintain order and justice. This approach of the *Mejelle* is seldom found in the other compilation of law.

As mentioned above, contract is a complex legal discipline both in its jurisprudential foundation and in its practical function. Intellectually, it is perhaps the most rewarding field of the law in action. The mechanism of contract formation depends on the fundamental conception of contract(s) under Islamic law, its interrelation with other modes whereby an obligation may be generated, the extent of the freedom of the parties and the grouping of contracts according to different classifications, of the close interaction of all these factors.

Historical Evolution of Contract in Islamic Law

As for the evolution of the law of contract, Islamic law of contract, unlike other legal systems, starts with Quranic verses which already contain both the rudiments of several types of nominate contracts as well as certain contractual maxims of general import. Thereafter, the traditions supplement the Quranic groundwork. The jurists in all Islamic Schools of law later developed the principles of contract. In the Quran, all in all, there are only over forty verses on a dozen types of commercial contract. Apart form one important verse on performing contract that is Quran 5:1 which enjoins believers to 'keep faith contracts' (awfu bi al-'uqud), and the three verses with a common theme of 'keeping promise', nonetheless, there are few verse which reveal a relatively advances stage of commercial contracts, such as sale and hire, charges in rem of personal guarantee as security fiduciary contracts such as deposit and the like. The whole idea of having a contract is to satisfy the consent of both parties to a contract and it seems, not only in Islamic legal system but also in other legal system, contract is the best available means to reflect the intention an accordingly the consent of the parties. To this effect, the Quran has already prescribed on the believers "not to devour your assets among yourself in vanity, except in trading by your consent". In addition, the Prophet (PBUH) is reported to have said that "The property of a Muslim is not licit for others to enjoy unless by his consent".

In any case, until the 19th century, no definition of contract is to be found in the treatises of Islamic law. This is because Islamic law never developed a general theory of contract. Instead, the overwhelming majority of Muslim jurist have focused on the contract of sale which they regarded as the model for all sorts of contracts. However, the Islamic Civil Law Codification which took place in the 19th century, namely both the Majallah al-Ahkam al-'Adliyyah and Murshid al-Hayran (the 1891 Egyptian version of the Ottoman's Majallah), started to give a precise definition to a contract. The Majallah, for instance, describes contract as a little contracting parties obligating themselves with regards a given matter and binding themselves together with the same as result of connecting an offer with an acceptance. Also according to the Majallah, contracting is the connection of an offer with an acceptance in a lawful manner which marks its effect on the subject of the connection.

Essential Elements of a Valid Contract

For a valid contract to take place in Islamic law, certain conditions are to be met. From the foregoing definition of the contract, it appears that a valid contract bases itself on six elements, namely the offeror and offeree; offer and acceptance; and the subject matter and the consideration. As for the parties to a contract, they must be legally competent to enter into a contract. The competence to transact is Islamic law is measured largely by two aspects, namely prudence and puberty as revealed in the Quran 5:4, "Prove orphans till they reach the marriageable age; then if you find them if sound judgment, deliver over unto them their fortune". With reference to an expression of both offer and acceptance, Islamic law of contract recognises both express contracts as well as what has been described as contract by conduct. It presupposes the making of an offer either orally by writing or by conduct. In certain cases, acceptance may also be implied from a party silence. However, Islamic law is distinct from other legal systems that it insists on the session of contract (majlis al-'aqd) in the sense that both the offer and acceptance are to be jointly connected in one single session without any gap in time or place. Therefore, the session occurs in any natural place where the parties meet to form their agreement. The session therefore creates the essential unity of the time and place necessary for the dual declarations of intention and consent.

Based on the above prescription which is agreeable to all schools of law, it may be said that certain interruptions during the session such as stopping to pray, or discussing other subjects, changing positions or attitudes, or even falling asleep are held to terminate the majlis and therefore the offer. Also under this principle of law, the acceptance should be immediate. However, before the offeree gives his acceptance, the offeror may withdraw his offer. Again, another provision of law which is attached to Islamic law is the notion of khiyar al-majlis *i.e.,* right to revoke the concluded offer and acceptance, provided both the parties are still available in the session of the contract left the session, the right to do so ceases to exit. As there are various interpretations surrounding the exact meaning of majlis or session of contract, the present writer, based on certain arguments, is more inclined to appeal to customary practice of any society to decide on the separation from the session of contract.

Pertaining to both offer and acceptance, classical Islamic law seemed to insist on the notion of contracts inter presenters in the sense that the contracting parties should hear other's declaration which is, it is respectfully submitted, devoid of legal relevance. The writer's opinion is that contracts inter absentees by means of representatives or modern communication systems such as the telephone, telex, fax, e-mail, letter are equally valid provided they are performed in one single session of contract.

As for the subject matter of contract, both the item and consideration, Islamic law stresses on the following matters, *i.e.,* lawfulness, existence, deliverability and precise determination. Lawfulness requires that the object must be lawful, that is something which is permissible to trade. It must be of legal value that is, its subject matter (mahall) and the underlying cause (sabab) must be lawfull; and it must not be proscribed by Islamic law, nor a nuisance to public order or morality. Also inherent in the lawfulness of the object is the condition that the object must be legally owned (or authorised) by the parties to a contract. The issues of existence presuppose that the object of a contract must be in existence at the time of contract. Thus, it is illegal for example to sell fetus. Delivery, on the other hand, indicates that the object must be capable of certain delivery. The classical jurists therefore, prohibit the sale of a camel which has fled a bird in the air or a fish in water. Finally, the object of a contract must be determined precisely as to its essence, its quantity and its value.

As for the consideration of price, Islamic law does not restrict it to a monetary price, but it may be in the form of another commodity. The Islamic prohibition against uncertainty requires that the price must be in existence and determined at the time of the contract and cannot be fixed at a later date with reference to the market price, nor can it be left subject to determination by a third party. In contract of money-exchange (sarf), the rule of riba must be adhered to render the contract valid.. May be spot or in the future.

The capability of the parties to contracts is of prime importance for the validity of the contract. In Islamic law, no person can validly conclude a legal transaction without first having attained physical and intellectual maturity that being the equivalent of majority to enjoy full capacity, a person, whether male or female, should attain physical puberty (bulugh) and enjoy sound judgment known also as prudence (rushd) in his or her judgment. The Shafi'i school of law adds a third requisite for majority and that is sound judgment in regard to religion. Puberty is attained for boys and girls with *(a)* the appearance of coarse hair around the sexual parts of the body al though this sign is not given any significance by the Hanafis with *(b)* vouluntary or incoluntary emission of the seminal fluid or with *(c)* the attainment of a given age except for Malik himself (not his school), who do not consider age as indicative of puberty.

Other signs of puberty particular to girls are menstruation and pregnancy. As mentioned above, for the majority of scholars prudence (rushd) equates to sound judgment in financial matter. As for the argument of the Shafi'is, this is weak simply because an impious Muslim might well be of sound judgment with regard to business matters. In brief, a person is deemed of age and enjoys full capacity. However, between infancy and majority a minor will normally reach the age of discernment or age of reason (sinn al-tamyiz) admittedly being six or seven Hanafis and Malikis give value to some transaction performed by a discerning minor; the authorise the discerning minor to conclude contracts fully beneficial, such as acceptance of gifts of bequests without his guardian's authorization. He is forbidden to conclude fully detrimental contracts such as granting loans or guarantees, whereas contracts which could end up by being either beneficial of detrimental, are subject to the guardian's ratification. Under Hanbali teaching a minor, whether discerning or not, cannot enter any kind of financial transactions but the contracts are valid with the approval of the guardian. Shafi'i have disapproved the contracts of a minor out rightly.

Apart from this general requirement of the legal capacity to enter into any kind of contract, Islamic law also imposes certain legal interdictions in the interest of third parties. The third party may confirm or annul the disposition of a person who is interdicted from disposing of his property. Therefore, the insolvent (al-muflis) is interdicted from disposing of his property by the judge in the interest of his creditors. Also, a person ill with death sickness is interdicted in the interests of person's heirs or creditors.

Classification of Contract

Contract, from an Islamic legal perspective is conceptually divided into two main categories, namely *(i)* unilateral and *(ii)* bilateral contract. While the former is gratuitous in character and does not require the consent of the recipient, the latter is more bound to strict rulings and guideline since it requires the consent of both the parties to a contract. Also what is normally 'tolerated' in unilateral contract, would not necessarily be the case in bilateral contract. Therefore, the (strict) conditions required for both the offeree and the subject matter of the bilateral contract would cease to apply in an unilateral contract. Unilateral contract comprises of transactions in favor of the recipient such as gift (hadiah, hibah), off-set of the debt (ibra), will (wassiyyat) endowment (waqf) and loan (qard).

The bilateral contract covers the remaining transactions in Islamic law which can be further divided into different classifications according to the very purpose and reason d'etre of the deal and agreement. In this regard, we may perhaps, classify these contracts to six classifications which are as follows:

1. Contracts of exchange ('uqud al-mu'awadat).
2. Contracts of security ('uqud al tawthiqat).
3. Contracts of partnership (shirkah).
4. Contracts of safe custody (wadi'ah).
5. Contracts pertaining to the utilisation of usufruct ('uqud al manfa'ah).
6. Contracts pertaining to do a work (*e.g.*, wakalah and ju'alah).

This classification is not meant to be exhaustive because in the future many new contracts with different features would possibly come to exist on the basis of the doctrine of permissibility (ibahah), as previously discussed, that would render all commercial transactions permissible in the absence of a clear prohibition. Nevertheless, the above classification seems to be quite comprehensive to cover all existing contracts found in Islamic fiqh literature. Mention should be made that each of these classifications consists of different transactions but contribute to the same purpose an reason d'etre of the underlying contract. For example, contract of exchange, will primarily concern trading as well as selling and buying activities inclusive of their subdivisions such as cash sale, deferred payment sale, deferred delivery sale, sale on order, sale on debt , sale on currency, auction sale and so on and so forth. Similarly other types of contracts also include many sub-divisions relevant to respective classification. For example, contract of security deal not only with with surety ship (kafalah) but also with pledge (rahn) and transfer of debt (hiwalah) because the very purpose of these sub contracts under contracts of security was to protect the interest of the parties to a contract particularly the interest of the party in whose favor the respective contracts are concluded. As far as contract pertaining to the utilisation of usufruct are concerned, it also cover a few sub-contract such as ijarah (hire and lease) ariyah (loan of tangible asset), waqf (endowment), qard (loan of money), etc. The contract of partnership (shirkah) also includes different types of partnership such as mudarabah (profit and loss sharing) musharakah (profit and loss sharing), sharikah al-abdan (partnership by contributing effort and skill), sharikah al-wujuh (partnership based on credit and reliability), muzara'ah (partnership in farming), musaqat (partnership in fruit trees), etc.

Reflection and Overview on the Classifications of Contracts

Although contracts in Islamic law of transactions are classified into different categories, it seems that the basic contract, in many cases and situations are the contract of exchange and utilisation of usufruct. The former presupposes the transfer of ownership while the later the transfer of usufruct of a property from one party to another. This is clear from the definition of both sale and hire in Islamic law Sale is defined as "the exchange of one commodity for another, one of which is called the object and the other the price", or "the transfer of ownership of property for another. Hire or ijarah is defined as the transfer of the usufruct for a consideration. Both these two contracts constitute the main activities of commercial activities because the remaining contracts are largely dependent on these two contracts.

Therefore, the law on sale as the contract par excellence and, next to it, on hire, was greatly expanded in Islamic law literature. These two contracts are the bases for the other contracts to take place. In other words, other contracts are dependant on these two contracts to exist and to give effect. On the contrary, these two contracts, relatively speaking, can be concluded between two parties without any need for other (supporting) contracts. For instance, hiwalah, kafalah and rahn cannot stand by itself in the sense that they are all dependent on the contract of exchange be it sale or lease/hire. In the case of hiwalah which means transferring a debt from one debtor to another, it cannot take place unless the debt relationship has already established between the transferee, the transferor and the principal creditor. The debt relationship, on the other hand, may take place either out of deferred payment sale or out of direct loan (qard) contract. Hence, it is obvious that hiwalah originates from the sale transaction (as well as from loan transaction) kafalah, rahn, etc.

This shows, inter alia, that contracts are inter-related to form a complete system of mu'amalah to ensure justice as well as to meet the needs of people which vary from one condition to another. Therefore, it is relevant to conclude that Islamic commercial law consists of many different types of contracts to suit different needs and circumstances. In other words, theoretically, Islamic commercial law would be able to satisfy the need of a person to buy a commodity on credit, or the need to have the guarantor against the third party, or the need to have the fund for business enterprise purposes, or the need to have in advance the capital to manufacture or produce agriculture produce or perhaps the need to have a transferee to settle the debt owed by a third party (transferor) and the like.

Contracts of Exchange (Mu'awadat)

The main contract of exchange in Islamic commercial law is the contract of sale. Sale, generally speaking, involves an exchange of a commodity for another commodity (barter trading) or of a commodity for money (sale) or of money for money (sarf). Interestingly enough, riba which is prohibited by Islamic law, originates or comes to exist from two types of exchange, namely unequal exchange of two ribawi or usurious commodities (riba al-fadl or riba al-buyu') or an exchange of money for money with different quantities (riba al-fadl) or without simultaneous transfer and immediate delivery (riba al-nasi'ah or riba al-duyun) or involving both possibilities which render the contract of exchange of money for money null and void based on both riba al-fadl as well as riba al-nasiah. The first impression that comes across to our mind is that both types of riba, while quite similar to both contracts of barter trading and currency exchange (sarf), are not similar in any way to an exchange of a commodity for money. This, among other reasons, makes the trading distinct and free from any element of interest. However, contracts of exchange dealing with barter trading and currency exchange are susceptible to riba elements and for this reason, Islamic law has relatively laid down more strict principles to ensure the legality of these contracts and most importantly to free these two contracts from both riba al-fadl and riba al-nasiah respectively. Trading activities *i.e.*, contracts of exchange of a commodity for money however, are relatively more exposed to the element of gharar, literally hazard or risk. In Islamic legal terminology, this includes the sale of an article of goods which is not present at hand; or the sale of an article of goods, the consequence or outcome of which is not yet known; or a sale involving risk or hazard where one does not know whether the commodity will later come to be or otherwise. Gharar may render the contracts of trading void or voidable. Several reasons were given for the prohibition of bay' al-gharar. Some of them were related to fraud since such a sale amounts to obtaining the property of others by selling unavailable goods and also the contract may lead to disputes and disagreements between the parties in the contract. While in Islamic law, an agreement must bring an immediate and certain obligation.

Therefore, it is not surprising to find that Islamic law has prohibited many pre-Islamic period's contracts of exchange because they were either uncertain or not known to one or both parties to the contract which may eventually lead to dispute and injustice. Such contracts are like bay' al-mulamasah, bay' al-hasat, bay' al-munabadah, bay' al muwafah, bay'muzabanah, bay al-mukhadarah, bay' al-muhaqalah, al-haml, bay'atan fi bay'ah or safqatan fi safqah, bay' al-kali bi al-kali, bay' wa salaf, etc. All of the above examples reflect clearly the hazardous elements that each of them contains and therefore, render the contract either void or voidable. From this brief introduction, we may infer that as far as barter trading and currency exchange are concerned, the principles of Islamic law which govern those transactions are mire concerned with the questions of equality between two items because these two types of exchange are vulnerable to riba element. On the contrary, the possibility of riba interference dies bit arise in the case of trading since trading activities are basically free from riba but are always exposed to exploitation and fraud. The question of equal amount and simultaneous transfer of the property being exchanged is irrelevant in trading activities simply because these two factors do not inflict any legal effect on the sale contract. This, the golden principle in trading is that the contract should not contain any element of either gharar or jahalah (lack of knowledge) because otherwise, the contract is deemed either void or voidable according to the degree of gharar or jahalah respectively. Also, for this reason, it is respectfully submitted, that the issues of the first possession of the property before the second sale qabd, the capacity to deliver the property, etc., are always questioned by, and debated amongst, the jurist only ill relation to trading (alone) because these two issues and the like are concerned with gharar and jahalah and not with riba.

On the contrary, the issues of gharar and jahalah, have no effect what so ever in certain contracts in the Islamic law of transactions because the nature of this type of contract does not require and demand a precise specification and identification of the property being transferred from one party to another. This is absolutely applicable to the contracts of gratuity ('uqud al-tabarru'at) such as hadiah, hibah, wasiyyat, etc. Why gharar affects trading and not gratuity contracts is a question worth of reflection. The immediate answer would be that trading differs from gratuity contracts because the former is a bilateral contract which requires an exact knowledge of the property to fulfill the requirement of legal consent while the latter does not require such knowledge since the consent of the recipient is not necessary. Again, the classification of contracts as given earlier would help the jurists to ascertain the legal position of the respective contracts in a given situation. Interestingly enough, the difference between the two types of contract such as between the contract of exchange and gratuity would induce different legal effects *e.g.*, khiyar or the right to revoke the contract. While khiyar (option) is undoubtedly part and parcel of the sale transaction, it finds no place in gratuity contract. Should we continue to examine the similarity and dissimilarity between one type of contract with another in issues pertaining to legal position, rights, obligations, liability, risk, merits, modus operandi, etc., we would have certainly produced so many pages on the topic which is not the intention of the present paper.

To be more specific, we should confine our present discussion to the contracts of exchange ('qud al-mu'awadat) which will include a variety of contracts which differ from one another on terms of specific legal requirements, rights, obligations and liabilities but common to each other in terns of the result of the contract, namely the transfer of ownership from one party to another. Therefore, the element common to all contracts under contracts of exchange is the transfer of the ownership and possession from one party to another. Should this be absent and lacking in a contract, the contract is no longer a contract of exchange. The relevant legal maxims which governs this situation is article 3 of the Majallah al-Ahkam al-'Adliyyah which reads as, "In contracts, attention is given to the objects and meaning, and not to the words and forms". The maxim clearly states that it is the object and aim of a transaction which will be determinative to the legal position of that transaction. The maxim cited is related to another maxim describing the function of intention in all aspects of Islamic law which reads as follows, "matters are determined according to intention". To illustrate the maxim governing the legal position of a contract as pointed out by article 3 of the Majallah, the drafters of the Majallah have cited the case of bay' al-wafa'. Bay' al-wafa' is basically a sale of commodity on the condition that the seller be allowed to get the commodity back upon paying its price. Therefore, in bay' al-wafa', the seller by returning the price, can demand back the thing sold, and the buyer, by returning the thing sold, can ask for the price to be reimbursed. Also, neither the seller nor the purchaser can sell to another a thing sold by bay' al-wafa'. This trahsaction is perceived by the Majallah as a pledge contract, not because of the words and forms used in the offer and acceptance but rather due to the intention and meaning as it is clearly expressed in the maxim cited earlier.

The case of bay' al-wafa' attracts the attention of the drafters of the Majallah since bay' al-wafa' is a transaction peculiar only to the Hanafi school of law and furthermore, the Majallah is primarily based on the Hanafi point of view. In addition, bay' al-wafa' is so unique because it is termed as a sale while in actual fact, as endorsed by the Majallah itself, it is rather a pledge (rahn) contract. That is to say, the relationship between the two parties to that contract could not be between the buyer and seller since the transfer of property and corresponding consideration is not final and ultimate. Rather, the contractual relationship would be between mortgagor (seller) and mortgagee (buyer) neither the seller nor the purchaser can sell to another a thing sold by bay' al-wafa'.

Contracts of exchange in the classical Islamic law of transactions, as mentioned earlier, include a number of contracts such as bay' al-musawamah, bay' al-murabahah, bay al-tawliyyah, bay' al-wadi'ah, al-bay' al-mua'ajjal, bay' al-salam, bay' al-istis'na', bay' al-muqayadah, bay' al-sarf, bay' al-muzayadah, etc. Apart from these types of sale, there are also other types of sale which are disputable among the jurists such as bay al-'arabiin, bay'al-'ayyinah and bay' al-dayn. In dealing with these different categories of sale contracts, the writer is more inclined to classify them into appropriate sections for the sake of clarification and distinction. The classification is based on certain factors which distinguish one contract of sale from another. Therefore, with special reference to the thing sold, sales are divided into four categories as follows:

1. sale of property to another person for a price and this is the most common category of sale and is consequently specifically called sale;
2. sale by exchange of money for money which is known as sarf transaction which consists of selling cash for cash;
3. sale by barter *i.e.*, exchange of object for object whereby neither of which is money payment; each of the two commodities constitute both the price and the object; and
4. sale by immediate payment against future delivery such as bay' al-salam (forward sale) and bay' al-istisna' (sale on order). The item of the sale is yet to exist in the future date.

From another perspective *i.e.*, the nature of profit agreed upon in the contract, sales are also divided into four categories as follows:

(i) Musawamah sale which is basically a sale by mutual consent completed and concluded through negotiations between the seller and buyer in which no reference is made to the original cost price. It is also a 'profit sale' but the actual cost price and the amount/percentage of the profit is unknown to the buyer because the seller is not bound, in musawamah sale, to disclose the cost price.

(ii) Murabahah sale which is the sate of a commodity for the price at which the seller has purchased it, with the addition of stated profit known to both the seller and buyer. In short, it is a cost-plus-profit sale in which the profit is expressly disclosed by the seller. From this, we can infer that murabahah sale in its original Islamic connotation is simply a sale. The only feature

distinguishing it from other kinds of sale is that the seller ill murabahah expressly tells the purchaser how much cost he has incurred and how much profit he is going to charge in addition to the cost. Therefore, if a person sells a commodity for a lump sum price or instalment basis without reference to the cost, this is not murabahah, even though he is earning some profit on his cost because the sale is not based on a 'cost-plus' concept. In this case, the sale is called musawamah. Due to speciality of murabahah, it has been considered by the jurist as a sale based on trust (amanah).

(iii) Tawliyyah sale which is a sale at cost price without any profit for the seller. It is similar to murabahah with reference to the basis of the sales, namely amanah.

(iv) Wadi'ah sale which takes place when the seller agrees to sell a commodity at a lower price than that of the cost price. Since the seller is selling the commodity at a lower price, it is also a trust sale.

According to the manner of payment, there are three possibilities of payment pertaining to a sale contract as follows:

1. Cash sale in which the purchaser is under obligation to settle the purchase price agreed upon when concluding a contract if the buyer could not settle the payment for one reason or another, the seller has a right of retaining the thing sold until he has received the payment of the price.
2. Deferred payment sale which is payable on installment basis. This is permissible provided the period thereof is definitely ascertained and fixed manner of payment is applicable to all types of sale except in the case of bay' al-salam.
3. Lump sum payment payable in the future. This manner of payment is also lawful provided the date of the payment is fixed in advance. Also, this manner of payment would be applicable to all types of sale with the exception of bay' al-salam.

4. Earnest money (bay' al-'arabun) in which advance payment of sum of money is made to the seller which constitutes part of the purchase price should the buyer decides to buy the good. Otherwise, the advance payment is forfeited to the seller.

According to the subject matter of the sale, it can be divided into three categories namely, sale of commodity (movable and immovable), currency (sari) and debt (dayn). As for the very purpose of sale contract, it may classified into two categories that are exclusively of exchange purposes and the other for exchange as well as for financing purposes.

Apart from the previous perspectives on which sales are usually classified, sales are also divided into a few categories according to the nature of the price whether is has been fixed from the very beginning or otherwise. This is however, the writer's personal reflection on certain contracts of sale available in the Islamic law of transactions. These categories are as follows:

(i) The price is mentioned by the offeror and accepted by the offeree. This is the practice in normal sale transaction whether it involves musawamah or murabahah or salam or istisna' and other types of sale with the exception of tawliyyah sale since the price offered in the latter must not go beyond the original cost price.

(ii) The price is mentioned by the buyer and later accepted by the seller, seller, in this context, is not bound by any 'offer' of the buyer but, on the contrary is bound to honor the highest price offered by the respective buyer or 'bidder'. This is called as bay' al-muzayadah or bay' man yazid or sale based on auctioning. In this transaction, the price will be fixed only by the highest offer made by the bidders.

(iii) The price in some sale transactions, is divided into two stages; the second payment is pending on the ultimate decision of the buyer to proceed with the contract or otherwise. This takes place in bay' al-'arabun (earnest money) in which the buyer agrees to purchase a

commodity and pays to the seller an amount of money in advance. If he decides to buy the commodity, the amount paid will be deducted from the purchase price, but if he declines or fails to buy the commodity, the advance payment is forfeited to the seller.

The fundamental basis of sale contract consists of one piece of property being exchanged for another. Offer and acceptance are also referred to as the fundamental basis of sale, since they imply exchange. As for the object, it must be in existence, deliverable and known to the purchaser. These conditions are applicable to many types of sales except in few contracts such as bay' al-salam and istisna'.

Contracts of Utilisation of Usufruct ('Uqud al-Manfa'at)

The above type contract is divided into two categories which are the transfer of the usufruct for a consideration and the transfer of the usufruct without a consideration. The former is a bilateral contract while the latter is not. The former is known as contract ijarah while the latter is known as 'ariyah contract. The details of these two contracts are as follows:

Contract of Ijarah (Transfer of Usufruct for a Consideration)

Ijarah is a word that conveys the sense of both hire and lease. Ijarah is of two kinds, namely use of corporeal property which may take one of three forms:

- Immovable property, such as land or premises.
- Merchandise, such as furniture, machinery, etc.
- Animals.

The second type of ijarah is personal service. The salient features of ijarah contract are as follows:

(i) The lessor must be the absolute owner of the thing or the agent of the owner of his natural or legal guardian.

(ii) The thing given for rent and the amount of rent should be fully and precisely known to both parties.

(iii) In a contract of hire, it is necessary to make known the use to which the thing hired is to be put, so as to avoid later dispute.

(iv) When land is taken for rent, the period must be fixed and the purpose for which it is rented specified.

(v) In hiring an artisan, the benefit should be made known by a statement of the nature and method of workmanship.

(vi) It is the responsibility of the lessor to maintain the property leased in such a way as to retain the benefit of the property.

(vii) If the lessee damages the property hired, the lessor can annul the lease on application to the court.

(viii) The lessee can sub-let immovable property but not movable property.

(ix) The thing hired should be treated as a trust in the hands of the user.

Ariyah (Lending for Gratuitous Use)

In addition to the above general rules, the contract of 'ariyah requires the following rules:

1. The lender may withdraw the loan whenever he wishes.
2. The thing lent must be capable of giving a benefit.
3. The thing lent for use must be defined.
4. The borrower becomes the owner of the benefit without giving any payment to the owner.
5. The maintenance of the thing borrowed for use is the responsibility of the borrower.
6. When lending for use is restricted as to time, place and nature of use, the restriction are to be observed.
7. The borrower cannot let or pledge the thing lent for use, the borrower must immediately return it.
8. When the lender demands the thing lent for use, the borrower must immediately return it.
9. The expense and care of returning a thing lent for use fall on the borrower.

Contracts of Security

Thus type of contract consists of three contracts which are hiwalah, kafalah and rahn explanation of each of the contracts is as follows:

(i) Hiwalah (Transfer of Debt)

Hiwalah means transferring a debt from one debtor (transferor) to another (transferee). Once the transferee has accepted the transfer of debt, the transferor would be released from any obligation. Therefore, as a consequence of the transfer of debt (hiwalah), unlike suretyship, the debtor who transfer his debt and his surety, if ally, are freed from their respective obligations. The creditor can now claim his debt only from the transferee. The transferee, after payment, has aright to claim the amount so paid from the transferor. In such a case, the transferor's claim from the transferee, of any, will be adjusted towards the claim. However, the transferee would be released from his liability in any of the following four situations:

(i) By payment of the debt.

(ii) By further transferring the debt to another person if the creditor accepts.

(iii) By cantonments by the creditor.

(iv) If the creditor dies and person who accepts the transfer is his heirs.

(ii) Rahn (Pledges)

A creditor, whether an individual or a financial institution, prefers to secure a loan either through personal surety or a pledge. Pledge or rahn is to make a property a security in respect of a right of claim, the payment for which may be taken from the value of the property. The main laws relating to pledge, inter alia, are as follows:

- The contract becomes irrevocable after the pledge is received by the pledgee.
- One pledge may be exchanged for another.
- The pledge may, on his own accord, all the contract.
- Two different creditors may take a common pledge from a single debtor. This pledge will secure the whole of the two debts.
- When a debt is partly paid off, it does not become necessary to return the part of the pledge equivalent to

it in full. The pledge has a right to hold the whole until the debt is paid.

- If the pledgor has destroyed or damaged the thing pledged, he must pay compensation. If the pledge has destroyed or damaged it, the amount of its value is struck off the debt.
- If the time for paying the debt has arrived, and the pledgor refuses to make payment, the pledge may approach the court to compel the pledgor to sell the thing pledged in order to pay the debt. On his refusal, the court may sell the pledge to pay the debt.

(iii) Kalafah (Suretyship)

Kalafah means to add an obligation to an existing obligation in respect of a demand for something. This may relate to a person, finance or act (performance). Kafalah relating to a person involves the production of the person for whom the kafalah (bail) has been given. Kafalah relating to finance implies an obligation. Kafalah relating to an act or performance as to ensure the performance of a certain act, the failure of which may render the surety liable and responsible. One important point to be stressed is that kafalah, unlike hiwalah, would not release the principal debtor in whose favour the contract is concluded because kafalah is only an obligation in addition to the existing obligation. Among other rules governing kafalah are as follows:

- It is lawful to become surety for surety.
- There may be more than one surety for a single obligation.
- If persons who are jointly indebted become surety for each other, each of them is liable for the whole debt.
- The discharge of the surety does not necessarily discharge the liability of the principal debtor concerned. The opposite scenario will be acceptable as far as the discharge is.
- If a delay is granted to the principal debtor for the payment of his debts, a delay is also granted to the surety principal debtor. But a delay given to the surety is not a delay given to the debtor.

CHAPTER

6

Islamic Fund and Asset Management

Shariah Compliant Equity Funds

Shari'ah Perspective

Unit Trusts are based on the concept that risks and rewards are shared by the investors, employing the expertise of professional managers. This is in conformity with Islamic partnership principles of musharakah and mudarabah and is already applied within the Islamic financial system.

1. Investment must be made in ethical sectors. In other words, profits cannot be generated from prohibited activities such as alcohol production, gambling, pornography etc.
2. Investing in interest (riba) – based financial institutions are not allowed.
3. All wealth creation should result from a partnership between an investor and the user of capital in which rewards and risks are shared. Returns in invested capital should be earned rather than be pre-determined.

Islamic Unit Trusts

The Islamic unit trust schemes are collective investment funds which offer investors the opportunity to invest in a diversified portfolio of Shari'ah – compliant securities which are managed by professional managers in accordance with the Shaṛi'ah. The Islamic unit trust schemes are required to additionally appoint a Shari'ah committee or a Shari'ah adviser to ensure that their operations are in accordance with Shari'ah.

The main objective of an Islamic Unit Trust is to invest in a portfolio of 'halal' (permissible) stocks which comply with the principles of the Shari'ah. Such 'halal' stocks will exclude companies involved in activities, products or services related to conventional banking, insurance and financial services, gambling, alcoholic beverages and non-halal food products.

The returns of the Islamic Unit Trust must also avoid the incidence of 'riba or usury interest through the process of cleansing or purification by the removal of such amounts representing the interest element. Such proceeds are normally donated to charities.

The common types of financial contracts and products that are used by Islamic financial institutions are recounted below:

1. *Mudarabah*: A contract in which all the capital of a venture is provided by the Unit Trust and the business expertise and management is the responsibility of the third party. Profits are divided between the third party and the Trust according to the terms of the contract.
2. *Murabaha*: A contract in which a third party wishing to purchase equipment or goods (primarily commodities) requests the Trust to purchase such items and charge them the cost plus a reasonable profit. The profits accrue to the Trust 3.
3. *Musharakah*: A joint venture in which both the Trust and the third party contribute funds, producing equity participation.
4. *Ijara and ijara wa iqtina*: A contract in which the Trust finances equipment, a building or an entire project for a third party against an agreed rental and the third party undertakes to make payments to the Trust which will eventually result in the ownership by the third party of the equipment or project. The difference in value

between the cost of the original finance provided and the total payments made by the third party accrues to the Trust. There is no doubt that investment in interest-bearing securities or businesses dealing in pork meat, alcohol, gambling and other activities prohibited by the Shari'ah cannot be acceptable. Profit in itself is not prohibited by the Shari'ah. Indeed, trade is encouraged, through which legitimate profit can be derived. The main objection against conventional business practices is that the profit on their transactions is primarily based on interest-bearing borrowing and lending.

Buying and selling company shares is a matter of investing and earning and there is no participation in management. This includes mergers, take-over, joint ventures and venture capital projects. Although there are differences of opinion among Muslim scholars about shareholding, those who have considered it most deeply generally hold the following opinion:

"If a company is not involved in the manufacture or sale of haram goods and its business is not based on interest or gambling, it is permissible for a Muslim to buy its ordinary shares and benefit from its dividends. However, buying its preference shares is not permissible.

"Sometimes objections are raised about the purchase of such companies' shares, from the Shari'ah point of view, on the ground that these companies borrow from banks, etc., on interest, but in these cases interest is paid rather than received, and so the element of interest is not included in the companies' profits. Doubts may be expressed that these companies open interest accounts with banks and include interest accrued on their deposits in their profits. But it can be argued that the amounts receivable from interest accounts are generally very small in comparison with the total profits and therefore rather insignificant, which is why the bulk of the profits may be accepted without hesitation.

"Besides this, keeping in view the evolutionary period through which the Islamic financial institutions are passing, there is scope to deal with non-Muslim companies to this extent, unless and until the Islamic Institutions become so strong that they are able to deal with non-Muslim institutions on their own terms only".

There are many financial products in conventional financial markets which are not interest-based, or where the element of interest could be eliminated. For example:

- Property funds and property investment trusts.
- Trading in commodities.
- Financial options and futures.
- Forward transactions in foreign currencies.
- General trade-financing transactions.

The Islamic Unit Trust may combine three important factors:

1. Conventional investment expertise.
2. Islamic finance expertise.
3. Shari'ah guidelines provided by Islamic religious scholars.

In this way, individual Muslim investors, Muslim corporate bodies and Islamic financial institutions can take part in the international markets and thus benefit from the growth of these markets.

Islamic Unit Trusts will give priority to equity investments in:

- Islamic banks and financial institutions'.
- Stock markets of Muslim countries.
- Companies managed under the Islamic system.

Shari'ah Principles for Investment Funds

Mudarabah Fund

In the Mudarabah fund the amount may be invested in a specific business activity on the basis of profit and loss sharing.

Equity Fund

In an equity fund the amounts are invested in the shares of joint stock companies. The profits are derived mainly through the capital gains by purchasing the shares and selling them when their prices are increased. Profits are also achieved by the dividends distributed by the relevant companies. If the main business of a company is not lawful in terms of Shari'ah it is not allowed for an Islamic Fund to purchase, hold or sell its shares, because it will entail the direct involvement of the shareholder in that prohibited business. Similarly the contemporary Shari'ah experts are almost unanimous on the point that if all the transactions of a company are in full conformity with Shari'ah which includes that the company neither borrows money on interest nor keeps its surplus in an interest bearing account, its shares can be purchased, held and sold without any hindrance from the Shari'ah side. But evidently, such companies are very rare in the contemporary stock markets. Almost all the companies quoted in the present stock market or in some way involved in an activity which violates the injunctions of Shariah Principles.

Murabaha Fund

In a Murabaha fund the amount is companies whose operations are on basis of murabaha where transactions are undertaken on a cost-plus basis. This kind of sale has been adopted by the contemporary Islamic banks and financial institutions as a mode of financing. They purchase the commodity for the benefit of their clients, and then sell it to them on the basis of deferred payment at an agreed margin of profit added to the cost. If a fund is created to undertake this kind of sale, it should be a closed-end fund and its units can not be negotiable in a secondary market. The reason is that in the in the case murabaha as undertaken by the present financial institutions, the commodities are sold to the clients immediately after their purchase from the original supplier, while the price being on deferred payment basis becomes a debt payable by the client. Therefore, the portfolio of murabaha does not own any tangible assets, rather it comprises of either cash or the receivable debts, and both these things are not negotiable, as explained earlier. If they are exchanged for money, it must be at par value.

Ijarah Fund

The Ijarah Fund will involve in companies dealing in the leasing of assets according to Shari'ah principles. The ownership of these assets remains with the Fund and the rentals are charged from the users. These rentals are the source of income for the fund which is distributed prorated to the investors.

Mixed Fund

Another type of Islamic Fund maybe of a nature where the subscription amounts are employed in different types of investments, like equities, leasing, commodities, etc. This may be called a Mixed Islamic Fund. In this case if the tangible assets of the Fund are more than 51 per cent while the liquidity and debts are less than 50 per cent the units of the fund may be negotiable. However, if the proportion of liquidity and debts exceeds 50 per cent, its units cannot be traded in according to the majority of the contemporary scholars. In this case the Fund must be a closed-end Fund.

Islamic Funds and Socially Responsible Investments

Shari'ah Committee

Islamic unit trust schemes must be supervised by a Shari'ah committee or Shariah adviser to ensure that the fund is managed and administered in accordance with Shari'ah principles. The Shari'ah Committee should function independently of trustee and portfolio manager. The following are some of the important Shari'ah supervisory functions enumerated by international Shari'ah scholar, Shaikh Yusuf Talal Delorenzo.

Portfolio Purification

Fiscal purification of earnings: income from interest-bearing investments should be deducted from total earnings.

Moral purification: the concept may be best understood in the context of the Qur'anic concept of 'enjoining the right and prohibiting what is wrong'. [3104, 110 and 114-7:157-9:71] Zakat: it is the moral duty of individual Muslim investor to pay zakat calculated as a proportion to their own personal wealth. Although there is debate on whether zakat should be paid on investments, the matter should be left to the individual.

Portfolio Selection: Screening Stocks

Scrutiny of stocks is one of the most important functions of Shari'ah Boards. If an Islamic fund subscribes to an Islamic index with a full Shari'ah supervisory board, then an independent supervisory board must oversee the choice of investments.

Portfolio Monitoring

Apart from selecting stocks, it is equally important to monitor them as business situations continually change. It is essentially that vigilance is required to ensure that the fund's portfolio remains within the prescribed Shari'ah criteria. Where a stock fails to comply with the criteria, then it is the Shari'ah supervisor's responsibility to verify the removal of the stock from the fund portfolio. If however, the fund subscribes to an Islamic index, then the Shari'ah supervisory board of the Islamic index will be responsible.

Working with Fund Management

Fund managers may not always be clear on the application of Shari'ah principles in certain situations or complex financial instruments and there is likely to be lapses and innocent mistakes with regard to non-compliance; when the fund manager is a non-Muslim the likelihood could be greater. The relationship of the Shari'ah Board and the fund management team is therefore equally important. For example, fund mangers may hold substantial cash waiting to be invested or they need to invest the cash in jurisdictions where non-interest bearing stocks are not available. The Shari'ah Board has a role to pay when it is a matter to avoid interest, or of purifying the interest that has accrued when no other course of action is available.

Monitoring of Fund Fees

The Board is strictly not required to be concerned fees charged by fund managers; it is essentially a business decision. Islam exhorts transparency in business dealings, hence the Shari'ah Board should ensure that investors are made aware of the fund's fees and how these are structured.

Monitoring Fund Documentation

All documentation requires making references to the Shari'ah and its interpretations. It is, therefore, important that the Shari'ah Board is involved in the preparation and review of all pertinent legal and business documentation.

Proposed Additional Requirements for Islamic Unit Trust Funds

While Islamic Unit Trust Funds require to appoint a Shari'ah Committee, in a consultation paper produced in August 2001 by the Malaysian Securities Commission proposed the following additional requirements:

1. Composition of Investment Committee Members should play a role in ensuring that the investments made by the Islamic trust fund are in line with Shari'ah principles. In this regard, the Investment Committee of the Islamic unit trust fund must comprise of at least two members who are Muslims. Furthermore, there will be no qorum for the purpose of the Investment Committee meeting unless one Muslim member is present. In other words, all meetings of the Investment Committee concerning an Islamic unit trust fund must comprise of at least a Muslim member.
2. Compliance Unit must include a compliance officer or an assistant who is a Muslim. The compliance officer or the assistant should be present at the Shari'ah committee meetings.
3. Additional Role, powers and duties of the Shari'ah Committee consultant require:
   (a) The Shari'ah Committee, or a company appointed to advise on Shari'ah matters) will appoint one representative to attend the Investment Committee meeting when discussing matters relating to the Islamic unit trust fund. The representative is expected to advise on matters related to Shari'ah principles.

(b) The Shari'ah committee/representative must undertake necessary measures to avoid any potential conflict of interest, when attending more than one Investment Committee meeting of Islamic unit trust funds managed by different management companies.

(c) The Shari'ah committee/representative responsible for scrutinising the fund's transaction report provided by the trustee must prepare a report to be included in the fund's annual report certifying that the fund has been managed and administered in accordance with Shari'ah principles.

(d) A Shari'ah committee member must also meet the following criteria:
- is not an undischarged bankrupt;
- has not been convicted for any offence arising out of criminal;
- proceeding;
- is of good repute;
- possess the relevant qualifications and expertise, particularly in Fiqh Muamalat and Islamic jurisprudence.

Islamic Indexes for Islamic Funds

The Dow Jones Islamic Markets (DJIM) is one of the important Islamic indexes and their approach Islamic screening is considered in this section by way of an example (Islamic indexes: the DJIM framework by Rushdi Siddiqi, Islamic Asset Management pp. 46-55, Euromoney Books 2006). Islamic screening takes place at three levels:

- Prohibited industries.
- Acceptable financial ratios.
- Monitoring, removal and replacement.

Parameters for Acceptable Industries

The first level of DJIM screening for Shari'ah – approved companies is divided into two parts. *First*, an Islamic investor may not purchase fixed-income securities, preferred shares, convertible notes or other similar instruments. The reason for this is that a predetermined rate of return is stipulated, while the principal is guaranteed. This clearly falls within the riba prohibition on interest-bearing loans, even if the primary business of the company (whose securities, shares or notes are tendered) is halal or in compliance with the Shari'ah law.

Secondly, an Islamic investor may not purchase the shares of companies whose primary or basic business is haram (unlawful), including (but not limited to): alcohol; tobacco; pork products; conventional financial services (banking, insurance, etc.); defence/weapons; entertainment (such as hotels, casinos or gambling, cinema, pornography and music). The majority of Shari'ah scholars and boards hold that these industries and their financial instruments are inconsistent with Shari'ah precepts and, hence, not suitable for Islamic investment purposes. While there is no universal consensus among contemporary Shari'ah scholars on the prohibition of tobacco companies and the defence industry, most Shari'ah boards have advised against investment in companies involved in these activities. Shari'ah scholars are obligated both morally and ethically to inform Muslims of things that are good, decent and beneficial, not only for themselves individually but also for humankind. They encourage Muslims to seek out and examine the merits of companies that, for example, have pro-environmental and pro-animal policies, or support their communities, or give voice to the disenfranchised, or that provide humanitarian services.

Revenue Breakdown

Once the negative primary business screen has eliminated the 'sin' sectors, the DJIM Shari'ah supervisory board next concentrates on quantifying the business revenue sources for a company. The objective is to quantify components of the company's revenue (including all the divisions or subsidiaries) or, if all the divisions or subsidiaries are in permissible lines of business, then all the revenue is acceptable. (Data vendors such as Worldscope and Factset, and company's annual reports and websites are the main source of information on the company's business description and revenue breakdown.) In quantifying business revenue, the funds may undertake the process of 'purification' to remove impermissible securities from the fund. The threshold set by the DJIM Shari'ah supervisory board is impermissible revenue of 5 per cant, so anything above that amount results in non-inclusion (or deletion at quarterly reviews) of the company.

Financial Ratios

What generally distinguishes Islamic (equity) investing from socially responsible investing (SRI) and faith-based investing (Christian and Catholic funds) is the emphasis on the balance sheet of the company in question. It should be noted that there are a number of references in the Bible to 'dealings against interest or usury' (for example, Exodus 22:25-6; Leviticus 25:35-37; Deuteronomy 23:19-20; Nehemiah 5:7; Psalms 15:5; Proverbs 28:8; and Ezekiel 18:8, 18:17 and 22:12). Their enforcement, however, is another issue.

Leverage

This is first level of DJIM financial screens examines the leverage (or gearing) ratios of the company in question. Contemporary Shari'ah scholars have allowed the acquisition of shares in a company with leverage that does not exceed one-third of equity, defined as market capitalisation or assets. This ruling is based on two principles. *First*, despite the serious sin committed by a borrower on the basis of interest, the loan so acquired becomes his own property. Secondly, a proportion less than one-third is understood in some cases to be minor. That one-third is representative of preponderance may be derived from a hadith, related by al-Bukari, in which Prophet Muhammad (pbuh) said: ...'Then a third. And a third is a great deal', when he was asked how much of one's estate a person may bequeath to some one other than the prescribed heirs. (It should be stated emphatically here that this formula is one that applies to investors interested in companies offering shares on the international market over which

Muslims have no control. It should not be understood as an endorsement of the practice, by Muslim-owned businesses, of interest-based borrowing).

The DJIM Shari'ah supervisory board has advised in favour of setting the debt/market capitalisation ratio requirement at less than 33 per cent. To reduce volatility, the DJIM uses a 12-month trailing average for market capitalisation. The FTSE Global Islamic Index Series uses debt/assets, while the KLSE Islamic index does not have a leverage screen. Using the market capitalisation method captures.

1. actual market valuation of the company, unlike assets which is an accounting entry;
2. market sector rotations; and
3. services/technology-oriented companies with significant goodwill, while the asset measure captures companies such as utilities that have hard assets.

The DJIM leverage screen deleted companies such as WorldCom (2001 second quarter), Tyco (2002 first quarter), Enron (2001 third quarter), Global Crossing (2001 second quarter) and others from the compliant universe before the accounting irregularities came into the public domain. Thus for analysts and managers, the leverage screen has become another 'tool in the tool box' for analysing companies, especially in down markets.

Cash Plus Interest-bearing Securities

The second level of DJIM financial screens attempts to ascertain the level of nonoperating interest income. General practice at most companies is that surplus monies will be deposited into interest-bearing accounts at banks, or used to purchase fixed-income securities (bonds, bills, notes) or certificates of deposits (CDs) of varying terms of maturity, or otherwise invested so that the principal is guaranteed and a predetermined rate of interest may be realised over a period of time. It should be noted that some companies engage in venture capital or partnership financing (similar to the Islamic musharakah instrument), such that they purchase equity shares in other companies. Obviously, dubious or tainted returns from fixed-income sources are considered haram on their own, but, as has already been explained, negligible amounts of such income will not prohibit the acquisition of shares in a company.

Such dubious income, however, must be kept to a minimum if the company is to conform to Shari'ah precepts. Some Shari'ah boards state that non-operating interest income/revenue (or sales) should not exceed 5 per cent, while other boards set a 10 per cent or even 15 per cent limit. Unlike the one-third provision, which is based on a hadith reference, the 5, 10 or 15 per cent is based rather on an interpretation of what is 'minor'.

The present DJIM cash screen-cash plus interest-bearing securities/market capitalisation of less than 33 per cent-has a high correlation to the previously used screen (non-operating interest income/revenue, or NOlI/R, of less than 5 per cent). An extensive study by Dow Jones Indexes, under the guidance of the DJIM subcommittee, showed that companies that pass the previous screen (NOlI/R of less than 5 per cent) also pass the present screen and vice versa. Furthermore, the present screen arguably provides more insight about a company. A company (for example, Comfort Group in early 2001) may have (low) NOlI/R of 0.45 per cent. While the cash plus interest-bearing securities/market capitalisation screen may be (high) at 32.28 per cent, implying that this company is not highly valued by the market as it has low market capitalisation and hence a high cash screen ratio. The previous NOlI/R of less than 5 per cent screen would not provide such an insight. When the percentage of haram income can be shown to have been kept to a minimum, it implies that the company is utilising its resources, labour and capital for enhancing productivity and not merely relying on passive (that is, fixed) or Haram sources of income. In this manner, the company's lawful returns are maximised.

The haram income must be calculated and 'purified by way of giving to charity, without the expectation on the part of the investor that such giving will in any way relieve him/

her of the responsibility to pay Zakat, or otherwise carry any religious benefit. The DJIM Shari'ah supervisory board is of the opinion that each Islamic fund should have its own Shari'ah-supervised purification methodology and formula, hence avoiding imposing its formula on other boards.

The FTSE Islamic Global Index does not have either an interest income or cash screen, but purifies all impermissible income. The KLSE National Shari'ah Index has an interest income/turnover screen, but does not quantify the percentage amount. Sheikh Mohamme'd Elgari, when asked about the non-operating interest income and cash plus interest-bearing securities screen in a DJIM Shari'ah sub-committee meeting, has admitted its limitations.

In my opinion no criteria is perfect. There wilt always be anomalies. The 5 per cent standard is no exception. Sometimes it fails to exclude certain companies whose assets are mostly interest based. In situations where [the] interest rate is very low (or negative like Japan) a company may have [a] big chunk of its assets as cash or semi-cash, yet interest earning is so low it passes the 5 per cent criterion. It will not pass the new criterion. For that criterion includes not 'interest earning' but the source of such interest earning, which is cash. On the other hand, there are cases where cash is low but interest earning is so high that it will pass this new criterion but will only be 'caught' by the old 5 per cent benchmark. Therefore, we should continuously try to improve these standards, taking into consideration that changes that are too frequent may not be advisable. This aspect of non-permissible earnings of companies is the most difficult part of the Islamic equity investment programme. It has always been the case, since inception. As we all know, purification is the most Shari'ah-solid part of the criteria. This is because it is the part that almost all jurists would agree on. Yet it has not been attended to by fund managers in a Shari'ah-satisfactory way. The reason is that it requires expertise (as well as time) that is usually not available at the fund manager level.

Liquidity Screen (Accounts Receivable in Relation to Total Assets)

As the business community becomes increasingly regionalised. Nationalised and globalised, the volumes of everyday corporate transactions have increased from millions to hundreds of millions of dollars. Given the size and complexity of these transactions, very few, if any, companies have the capability to make full cash payments. This is why companies (buyers) generally agree to pay in instalments over a period of time. Such payment agreements result in the selling companies maintaining accounts receivable on their balance sheets. The Shari'ah, however, only allows selling value for value, while prohibiting interest rate-based discounting. Hence, the indebted can only sell to himself and not to a third party. Islamic banks employ a similar financing tool-murabaha-which is a form of cost-plus financing for accounts receivable. For example, once a corporate buyer and seller agree on the terms and conditions for a purchase, the buyer will approach the Islamic bank for financing because he, the buyer, does not possess sufficient liquid funds to make an outright purchase. The Islamic bank will employ its due diligence procedures and, upon satisfaction, will purchase the product from the seller and then sell it to the buyer for a pre-agreed price on an instalment basis in which the bank's profits are built into the buyer's instalment purchase price. In this manner, Islamic banks offer a Shari'ah – compliant alternative to accounts receivable.

The Shari'ah allows investing in shares of companies in which the primary business activity is deemed lawful if the accounts receivable do not represent the majority (more than 50%) of total assets. Thus, if the primary business of the company is halal and the sale methodology for obtaining corporate revenue is through instalment payments, which may be deemed incidental or subordinate if the accounts receivable do not exceed 45 per cent of total assets, then investment in such a company will be permissible. It should be noted in this regard that if the receivables total more than 50 per cent, the majority of the company's dealings will actually be in money, and not in goods, services and assets. This position is consistent with the established and recognised Islamic juristic rule stating that what is not permitted independently may be permitted subordinately, cited in many contemporary fatwas. Therefore, if the accounts receivable do not exceed 45 per cent of total assets, consistent with the rule of majority determining ultimate judgement, an Islamic investor will not be prohibited from purchasing shares in such a company.

Review Process for Continued Compliance

Index providers generally review or rebalance the companies in their universe quarterly, semi-annually, annually or when corporate actions take place (mergers, bankruptcies, etc.), in order to remove illiquid or near insolvent companies and replace them with other companies from the same sector. This phenomenon results in many broker-dealers undertaking studies on companies to be deleted and added before the index provider actually makes the announcement. The companies in the DJIM are reviewed on a quarterly basis for continued compliance, while the companies in the FTSE Global Islamic Index Series and the KLSE Islamic Index are reviewed on a semi-annual basis. Generally, Shari'ah supervisory boards of Islamic mutual funds allow 30 to 60 days (some even 90 days) to remove a non-compliant company so as to minimize any adverse financial impact on the portfolio/fund. Consequential issues relating to company capital appreciation and dividends, post-deletion but pre-sale may need to also be taken into account. Most companies deleted in the quarterly review process are removed due to violation of the leverage screen. Many of the companies deleted are small and mid-capitalised companies, as opposed to large cap.

CHAPTER

7

Sukuk
Islamic Equivalent of Bond

Sukuk is an Arabic term plural of sakk, 'legal instrument, deed, check' for a financial certificate or termed as an Islamic equivalent of bond.

In Islam, fixed income or termed as interest (riba') bearing bonds are not permissible. Hence, Sukuk is considered as securities that comply with the Islamic law. Its investment principles prohibit the charging, or paying of interest. Financial assets that comply with the Islamic law can be classified in accordance with their tradability and non-tradability in the secondary markets. It is estimated that over RM 3, 500 billion of assets are managed according to Islamic investment principles.

Such principles form part of 'Shariah' (Islamic Law), but it is actually broader than its concept that it also encompasses the general body of spiritual and moral obligations and duties in Islam. Shariah-compliant assets worldwide are worth an estimated more than RM 1,750 billion and have grown at more between 8-12 per cent per year over the past decade, and in the Gulf and Asia, Standard and Poor's estimates that 20 per cent of banking customers would now spontaneously choose an Islamic financial product over a conventional one with a similar risk-return profile.

In classical period Islam sakk (sukuk) – which is cognate with the European root 'cheque' – meant any document representing a contract or conveyance of rights, obligations or monies done in conformity with the Shariah. Empirical evidence shows that sukuk were a product extensively used during medieval Islam for the transferring of financial obligations originating from trade and other commercial activities.

On the other hand, the essence of sukuk, in the modern Islamic perspective, lies in the concept of asset monetisation – the so called securitisation – that is achieved through the process of issuance of sukuk (taskeek). Its great potential is in transforming an asset's future cash flow into present cash flow. Sukuk may be issued on existing as well as specific assets that may become available at a future date.

The sukuk market valued for more than RM 175 billion (at the end of 2006) is due for an exponential rise in 2007 with every issue likely to be oversubscribed 5 to 6 times amid a fast growing interest in the western countries.

One point to note here that Shari'ah requires that financing should only be raised for trading in, or construction of, specific and identifiable assets. Trading in 'indebtedness' is prohibited and so the issuance of conventional bonds would not be compliant. Thus all Sukuk returns and cashflows will be linked to assets purchased or those generated from an asset once constructed and not simply be income that is interest based. For borrowers to raise compliant financing they will need to utilise assets in the structure (which could be equity in a 'tangible' company). It is worth noting that Equity financing is Shari'ah compliant and fits well with the risk/return precepts of Islam.

In the eyes of Islamic Jurisprudence or As Shariah, money is a measuring tool for value and not an 'asset' in itself, it requires that one should not take or receive income from money (or anything that has the genus of money) alone or in other words 'if money generates money per say' it will tantamount to riba'. This generation of money from money (simplistically interest) is 'Riba', and is forbidden. The implications for Islamic financial institutions are that the trading/selling of debts, receivables (for anything other than par), conventional loan lending and credit cards are not permissible.

Now come the question of uncertainty or 'Gharar' principle. It is widely understood to mean the uncertainty in the existence of an underlying asset in a contract and/or uncertainty in the contractual terms and this is an issue for Islamic scholars to address when considering the application of derivatives. Shariah also incorporates the concept of 'Maslahah' (Public interest), denoting that, if something is overwhelmingly in the public good, it may yet be transacted – and so hedging or mitigation of avoidable business risks, may fall into this category but there is still much discussion yet to come.

Sukuk are widely regarded as controversial due to their perceived purpose of evading the restrictions on Riba. Conservative scholars do not believe that this is effective, citing the fact that a sukuk effectively requires payment for the time-value of money. This can be regarded as the fundamental test of interest. Sukuk offer investors fixed return on their investments which is also similar in appearance to interest in that the investor's return is not necessarily dependent on the risks of that particular venture.

This seems to be similar but the fact is that it is not the same as the reality is that banks invest in assets and the return from these such as rent is evenly spread over the rental period and it is this stream of income which forms the basis of the 'fixed' income stream and return to investors. Furthermore, given that there is an asset in the background, there is more security for the investor which makes sukuk increasingly appealing to global investors including both Muslims and non-Muslims.

Sukuk financing can be quite mystifying for the outsider. A good analogy is one of ethical or 'Green' investing. Here the universe of investable securities is limited by certain criteria based on moral and ethical considerations. Islamic Finance is also a subset of the global market and there is nothing that prevents the 'conventional' investor from participating in the Islamic market.

Basics of Sukuk

Sukuk is popularly known as an Islamic or Sharia compliant 'Bond' whilst in actual fact, it is an asset-backed trust certificate.

- In its simplest form Sukuk is a certificate evidencing ownership of an asset or its usufruct.
- The Sukuk structures rely on the creation of a Special Purpose Vehicle (SPV).
- SPV would issue Sukuk certificates which represent for example the ownership of an asset, entitlement to a debt or to rental incomes or even accumulation of returns from various Sukuk (a hybrid Sukuk).
- The return provided to Sukuk holders therefore come in the form of profit from a sale, rental or a combination of both.
- Sukuk could be based on Mudaraba, Musharaka, Murabaha, Salam, Istisna, Ijara or hybrid of these.

Difference between Conventional Bond and Sukuk

- In its simplest form, a bond is a contractual debt obligation whereby the issuer is contractually obliged to pay to bondholders, on certain specified dates, interest and principal.
- In comparison, under Sukuk structure the Sukuk holders each hold an undivided beneficial ownership in the underlying assets. Consequently, Sukuk holders are entitled to share in the revenues generated by the Sukuk assets as well as being entitled to share in the proceeds of the realisation of the Sukuk assets.

Similarities between Conventional Bond and Sukuk

- *Marketability*: Sukuk are monetised real assets that are liquid, easily transferred and traded in the financial markets.

- *Rateability*: Sukuk can be easily rated.
- *Enhanceability*: Different Sukuk structures may allow for credit enhancements.
- *Versatility*: the variety of Sukuk structures (as many as over 27 possibilities) allow for: structuring across legal and fiscal domains, fixed and variable income options etc.

Issuing of Sukuk Involves a Number of Steps Like

- Preparing a detailed feasibility study (stating clear objectives to be achieved from the proposed Sharia-compliant business) and setting up of general framework and organizational structure to support the issuance process.
- Working out an appropriate Sharia structure to achieve the set objectives in compliance with Sharia.
- Arranging lead manager(s) to underwrite the Sukuk issue.
- Arranging legal documentation around the agreed Sharia structure (both from the Issuer's as well as arranger's perspective).
- Setting up the SPV to represent the investors (Sukuk holders).
- Putting the Sukuk into circulation.

Role of Sharia Advisors in Sukuk

- Sharia advisor (Sharia scholars or Sharia advisory firms with recourse to Sharia scholars) have a significant role to play. Amongst others, following may be listed as examples.
- Advising on proposed Sukuk structure and suggest a Sharia structure which otherwise fulfils the set economic aims.
- Working closely with legal counsel of the issuer to ensure that the legal documents are in line with Sharia requirements.
- Working closely with legal counsel of the arranger to ensure that the legal documents are in line with Sharia requirements.

- Issuing Fatwa on the whole Sukuk deal before the same can be put into circulation.

Sukuk in the Context of UK and Europe

- UK is all set to introduce new framework to support the issuance of Sukuk, through parliamentary legislation. Treasury minister, Ed Balls, has been quoted in media recently: "We are looking to place domestic Sukuk on the same footing as conventional products".
- It is indeed an encouraging step by the UK. But it is important that such a framework is designed involving industry practitioners with experience in Sukuk issues.
- In sum, future of Islamic finance (including Sukuk) is becoming more and more viable in the UK and wider europe.

Model of a Classic Sukuk Structure

Over the last few years there has been a dramatic growth in the use of Islamic finance techniques in raising capital that complies with the requirements of Shari'a law.

According to recent reports assets invested in an Islamic, Shari'a compliant, manner are now estimated to exceed US$250 billion with the pool of money held by Muslim investors estimated at US$1.5 trillion (and growing rapidly with high oil prices).

The growth of the Sukuk market, which only opened in 2002 with the Malaysian government US$600 million Sukuk issue, is a prime indicator of this trend. By 2004, US$6.7 billion of capital was raised through the issue of Sukuks and in the first six months of 2005 the total raised reached US$6.2 billion.

Under the Koran, interest (riba) earned on money (for example, a loan) is forbidden, but many other types of finance are allowed. The basic principle behind the Sukuk is that the holder has an undivided ownership interest in a particular asset and is therefore entitled to the return generated by that asset. The classic Sukuk structure involves an acquisition of a property asset by a special purpose company (SPC) established in a tax neutral jurisdiction. The company funds itself by the issue of Sukuk, declaring a trust in favour of the Sukuk holders. The Sukuk holders receive a return based on the rental income of the asset, taking the credit risk of the underlying lessee. There is a number of accounting and tax consequences which can arise when a UK property is transferred to a UK based SPC but these are beyond the scope of this article.

Increasing Interest

The growth in the Sukuk market is due to the confluence of a number of factors ranging from the geopolitical impact of the 9/11 atrocities to a more general interest in developing Shari'a compliant products and structures. The fundamental drivers behind the Sukuk market are the same as those for the conventional securities market as it aims to:

- Broaden the pool of investors.
- Spread risk away from financial institutions.
- Disintermediate the link between investors and borrowers.

Although the market is relatively small, the excess liquidity currently being pumped into Gulf economies means that another pool of investment funds is becoming available to corporate treasurers. As the market is developing rapidly and the jurisprudence from the Islamic scholars is becoming more settled, the issue costs for a Sukuk structure continue to fall. The TCIP (Trust Certificate Issuance Programme) established by the Islamic Development Bank (IDB) in May 2005 marks a further step in the development of the Sukuk market with the IDB able to use some of the financial assets on its balance sheet to underpin Sukuk issues under a medium term note (MTN) like programme structure. The TCIP structure is similar to that outlined above with the underlying assets being a mixture of ijara (lease), murabaha (instalment sale) and istisna'a (conditional sale) contracts.

Eligible Assets

The main stumbling block for accessing the Sukuk market is the availability of underlying assets that generate a Shari'a compliant income stream. An interest-derived income stream will not be eligible for inclusion in a Sukuk, but a rental-based income stream (whether from real estate or movable property) is ideal. The most popular asset class to date is real estate where rental income can be generated to provide cash flow returns to holders and repurchase obligations can be entered into to ensure principal repayments on the scheduled maturity dates. Other eligible assets have included aircraft, car fleets, pipelines and large air conditioning units.

Enforceability

Before being brought to market any Sukuk will need a declaration or opinion from Shari'a scholars that the relevant transaction complies with Shari'a law. There has been a degree of confusion as to the interplay between compliance with Shari'a law and with the enforceability of the relevant contracts. Recently, in Shamil Bank of Bahrain EC v Beximco Pharmaceuticals Ltd and Ors, the Court of Appeal held that an Islamic financing agreement which was expressed to be governed by both English and Shari'a law was governed by English law. The court held that the question of whether or not a contract was Shari'a compliant does not have a bearing on its enforceability. This confusion can of course be minimised by clear drafting.

The Future

It is expected that there will be continued strong growth in the Sukuk market. There is increasing standardisation of Sukuk documents in the marketplace which will drive costs down and improve the competitiveness of these instruments.

Islamic Bonds (Sukuk): Its Introduction and Application

The use of Sukuk or Islamic securities have become increasingly popular in the last few years, both as a means of raising government finance through sovereign issues, and as a way of companies obtaining funding through the offer of corporate sukuk.

Beginning modestly in 2000 with total three sukuk worth $336 millions the total number sukuk by the end of

2006 has reached to 77 with over US$ 27 billion funds under management. By the end of 2007 the total figure is expected to exceed US$35 billion.

Sukuk has developed as one of the most significant mechanisms for raising finance in the international capital markets through Islamically acceptable structures. Multinational corporations, sovereign bodies, state corporations and financial institutions use international sukuk issuance as an alternative to syndicated financing.

What is Sukuk

Sukuk in general may be understood as a shariah compliant 'Bond'. In its simplest form sukuk represents ownership of an asset or its usufruct. The claim embodied in sukuk is not simply a claim to cash flow but an ownership claim. This also differentiates sukuk from conventional bonds as the latter proceed over interest bearing securities, whereas sukuk are basically investment certificates consisting of ownership claims in a pool of assets.

Sukuk (plural of word sak) were extensively used by Muslims in the Middle Ages as papers representing financial obligations originating from trade and other commercial activities. However, the present structure of sukuk are different from the sukuk originally used and are akin to the conventional concept of securitisation, a process in which ownership of the underlying assets is transferred to a large number of investors through certificates representing proportionate value of the relevant assets.

Sukuk and Bond

A bond is a contractual debt obligation whereby the issuer is contractually obliged to pay to bondholders, on certain specified dates, interest and principal, whereas, the sukuk holders claims an undivided beneficial ownership in the underlying assets. Consequently, sukuk holders are entitled to share in the revenues generated by the sukuk assets as well as being entitled to share in the proceeds of the realisation of the sukuk assets.

A distinguishing feature of a sukuk is that in instances where the certificate represents a debt to the holder, the certificate will not be tradable on the secondary market and instead is held until maturity or sold at par.

Accounting and Auditing Organization for Islamic Financial Institutions (AAOIFI) defines sukuk as being:

"Certificates of equal value representing after closing subscription, receipt of the value of the certificates and putting it to use as planned, common title to shares and rights in tangible assets, usufructs and services, or equity of a given project or equity of a special investment activity".

In 2000 total size of the sukuk was only US$ 336 million with no sovereign sukuk in the market. We can see from the above table that the size of total sukuk issued in 2001 was only US$ 336 million and in a short span of just six year the total size of sukuk has crossed US$ 27 billion. The growth achieved in 2003 has been most impressive at 483 per cent. In 2006 also total growth achieved by sukuk is 122 per cent.

Benefits and Features

Tradable Shariah – compliant capital market product providing medium to long-term fixed or variable rates of return. Assessed and rated by international rating agencies, which investors use as a guideline to assess risk/return parameters of a sukuk issue.

- Regular periodic income streams during the investment period with easy and efficient settlement and a possibility of capital appreciation of the sukuk.
- Liquid instruments, tradable in secondary market.
- Uses of Sukuk Funds.

The most common uses of sukuk can be named as project specific, asset-specific, and balance sheet specific.

(a) Project-specific Sukuk

Under this category money is raised through sukuk for specific project. For example, Qatar Global sukuk issued by the Government of Qatar in 2003 to mobilise resources for the construction of Hamad Medical City (HMC) in Doha. In this case a joint venture special purpose vehicle (SPV), the Qatar Global sukuk QSC, was incorporated in Qatar with limited liability. This SPV acquired the ownership of land parcel, that was registered in the name of HMC. The land parcel was placed in trust and Ijara-based Trust Certificates (TCs) were issued worth US$700 million due by October 2010. The annual floating rate of return was agreed at LIBOR plus 0.45 per cent.

(b) Assets-specific Sukuk

Under this arrangement, the resources are mobilise by selling the beneficiary right of the assets to the investors. For example, the Government of Malaysia raised US$ 600 million through Ijara sukuk Trust Certificates (TCs) in 2002. Under this arrangement, the beneficiary right of the land parcels has been sold by the government of Malaysia to an SPV, which was then re-sold to investors for five years. The SPV kept the beneficiary rights of the properties in trust and issued floating rate sukuk to investors. Another example of Asset-specific sukuk is US$250 million five-year Ijara sukuk issued to fund the extension of the airport in Bahrain. In this case the underlying asset was the airport land sold to an SPV.

(c) Balance Sheet-specific Sukuk

An example of the balance sheet specific use of sukuk funds is the Islamic Development Bank (IDB) sukuk issued in August 2003. The IDB mobilised these funds to finance various projects of the member countries. The IDB made its debut resource mobilization from the international capital market by issuing US$ 400 million five-year sukuk due for maturity in 2008.

Types of Sukuk

Sukuk can be of many types depending upon the type of Islamic modes of financing and trades used in its structuring. However, the most important and common among those are ijarah, shirkah, salam and istisna. Among the fourteen eligible sukuks identified by the AAOIFI, following are more common:

1. *Mudaraba Sukuk*

These are investment sukuk that represent ownership of units of equal value in the Mudaraba equity and are registered in the names of holders on the basis of undivided ownership of shares in the Mudaraba equity and its returns according to the percentage of ownership of share. The owners of such sukuk are the rabbul-mal. (AAOIFI). Mudarba sukuk are used for enhancing public participation in big investment projects.

Following are the salient features of mudarba sukuk:

(i) Mudarba sukuk (MS) represent common ownership and entitle their holders share in the specific projects against which the MS has been issued.

(ii) The MS contract is based on the official notice of the issue of the prospectus which must provide all information required by shariah for the Qirad contract such as the nature of capital, the ratio for profit distribution and other conditions related to the issue, which must be compatible with shariah.

(iii) The MS holder is given the right to transfer the ownership by selling the deeds in the securities market at his discretion. The sale of MS must follow the rules listed below:

- *(a)* If the mudarba capital, before the operations of the project, is still in the form of money, the trading of MS would be like exchange of money for money. In that case the rules of bay al-sarf would be applied.
- *(b)* If muqarda capital is in the form of debt then it must satisfy the principles of debt trading in Islam.
- *(c)* If capital is in the form of combination of cash, receivables, goods, real assets and benefits, trade must be based on market price evolved by mutual consent.

(iv) The Manager/SPV who receives the fund collected from the subscribers to MS can also invest his own fund. He will get profit for his capital contribution in addition to his share in the profit as mudarib.

(v) Neither prospectus nor MS should contain a guarantee, from the issuer or the manager for the fund, for the capital or a fixed profit, or a profit based on any percentage of the capital. Accordingly:

(a) The prospectus or the MS issued pursuant to it, may not stipulate payment of a specific amount to the MS holder,

(b) The profit is to be divided, as determined by applying rules of shariah; that is, an amount access of the capital, and not the revenue or the yield, and

(c) Profit and Loss account of the project must be published and disseminated to MS holders.

(iv) It is permissible to create reserves for contingencies, such as loss of capital, by deducting from the profit.

(vii) The prospectus can also contain a promise made by a third party, totally un-related to the parties to the contract, in terms of legal entity or financial status, to donate a specific sum, without any counter benefit, to meet losses in the give project, provided such commitment is independent of the mudarba contract.

On the expiry of the specified time period of the subscription, the Sukuk holders is given the right to transfer the ownership by sale or trade in the securities market at his discretion.

Steps involved in the structure:

- Mudarib enters into an agreement with project owner for construction/commissioning of project.
- SPV issues sukuk to raise funds.
- Mudarib collects regular profit payments and final capital proceeds from project activity for onward distribution to investors.
- Upon completion, Mudarib hands over the finished project to the owner.

Mudaraba Sukuk in Practice

Shamil Bank of Bahrain raised 360 million Saudi Riyal investment capital through the Al Ehsa Special Realty

Mudaraba, representing an investment participation in a land development transaction with a real estate development company in the Kingdom of Saudi Arabia. The investment objective of the Mudaraba is to provide investors with annual returns arising from participation in the funding of a land financing transaction Profits due to investors will be accrued on the basis of returns attained from investing the subscriptions.

2. *Musharaka Sukuk*

These are investment sukuk that represent ownership of Musharaka equity. It does not differ from the Mudaraba sukuk except in the organization of the relationship between the party issuing such sukuk and holders of these sukuk, whereby the party issuing sukuk forms a committee from the holders of the sukuk who can be referred to in investment decisions (AAOIFI).

Musharaka Sukuk are used for mobilising the funds for establishing a new project or developing an existing one or financing a business activity on the basis of partnership contracts. The certificate holders become the owners of the project or the assets of the activity as per their respective shares. These Musharaka certificates can be treated as negotiable instruments and can be bought and sold in the secondary market.

"These are certificates of equal value issued with the aim of using the mobilised funds for establishing a new project, developing an existing project or financing a business activity on the basis of any partnership contracts so that the certificate holders become the owners of the project or assets of the activity as per their respective shares, with the Musharaka certificates being managed on the basis of participation or Mudaraba or an investment agency." (AAOIFI Standard 17, 3/6).

Steps involved in the structure:

Corporate and the Special Purpose Vehicle (SPV) enter into a Musharaka Arrangement for a fixed period and an agreed profit-sharing ratio. Also the corporate undertakes to buy Musharaka shares of the SPV on a periodic basis.

- Corporate (as Musharik) contributes land or other physical assets to the Musharakaa.
- SPV (as Musharik) contributes cash *i.e.,* the issue Proceeds received from the investors to the Musharaka.
- The Musharaka appoints the Corporate as an agent to develop the land (or other physical assets) with the cash injected into the Musharaka and sell/lease the developed assets on behalf of the Musharaka.
- In return, the agent (i.e. the Corporate) will get a fixed agency fee plus a variable incentive fee payable.
- The profits are distributed to the sukuk holders.
- The Corporate irrevocably undertakes to buy at a pre-agreed price the Musharaka shares of the SPV on say semi-annual basis and at the end of the fixed period the SPV would no longer have any shares in the Musharaka.

Musharaka Sukuk in Practice

US$550 million sukuk transaction for Emirates airline, the seven-year deal was a structured on a Musharaka contract. The Musharaka or joint venture was set up to develop a new engineering centre and a new headquarters building on land situated near Dubai's airport which will ultimately be leased to Emirates. Profit, in the form of lease rentals, generated from the Musharaka venture will be used to pay the periodic distribution on the trust certificates.

Sitara Chemical Industries Ltd, a public limited company, made a public issue of profit-and-loss sharing based term finance certificates (TFC's) worth Rs. 360 million which were subscribed in June 2002. The TFC's had a fixed life tenor of five years and profit and loss sharing was linked to the operating profit or loss of the Chemical Division of the company.

Kuwait Finance House (KFH), Liquidity Management Centre (LMC) and Al Muthanna Investment Company (MIC), the mandated lead arrangers launched US$ 125 million Lagoon City Musharaka sukuk to support the Lagoon City residential and commercial real estate development as part of Kheiran Pearl City project.

3. *Ijara Sukuk*

These are sukuk that represent ownership of equal shares in a rented real estate or the usufruct of the real estate. These sukuk give their owners the right to own the real estate, receive the rent and dispose of their sukuk in a manner that does not affect the right of the lessee, *i.e.,* they are tradable. The holders of such sukuk bear all cost of maintenance of and damage to the real estate. (AAOIFI).

Ijarah sukuk are the securities representing ownership of well defined existing and known assets tied up to a lease contract, rental of which is the return payable to sukuk holders. Payment of ijarah rentals can be unrelated to the period of taking usufruct by the lessee. It can be made before beginning of the lease period, during the period or after the period as the parties may mutually decide. This flexibility can be used to evolve different forms of contract and sukuk that may serve different purposes of issuers and the holders.

Features of Ijarah Sukuk

1. It is necessary for an ijarah contract that the assets being leased and the amount of rent both are clearly known to the parties at the time of the contract and if both of these are known, ijarah can be contracted on an asset or a building that is yet to be constructed, as long as it is fully described in the contract provided that the lessor should normally be able to acquire, construct or buy the asset being leased by the time set for its delivery to the lessee (AAOIFI, 2003: 140-157). The lessor can sell the leased asset provided it does not hinder the lessee to take benefit from the asset. The new owner would be entitled to receive the rentals.
2. Rental in ijarah must be stipulated in clear terms for the firs term of lease, and for future renewable terms, it could be constant, increasing or decreasing by benchmarking or relating it to any well-known variable.
3. As per shariah rules, expenses related to the corpus or basic characteristics of the assets are the responsibility of the owner, while maintenance expenses related to its operation are to be borne by the lessee.

4. As regards procedure for issuance of ijarah sukuk, an SPV is created to purchase the asset(s) that issues sukuk to the investor, enabling it to make payment for purchasing the asset. The asset is then leased to third party for its use. The lessee makes periodic rental payments the SPV that in turn distributes the same to the sukuk holders.
5. Ijara sukuk are completely negotiable and can be traded in the secondary markets.
6. Ijara sukuk offer a high degree of flexibility from the point of view of their issuance management and marketability. The central government, municipalities, awqaf or any other asset users, private or public can issue these Sukuk. Additionally, they can be issued by financial intermediaries or directly by users of the leased assets.

Steps involved in the structure:

- The obligator sells certain assets to the SPV at an agreed pre-determined purchase price.
- The SPV raises financing by issuing sukuk certificates in an amount equal to the purchase price.
- This is passed on to the obligator (as seller).
- A lease agreement is signed between SPV and the obligator for a fixed period of time, where the obligator leases back the assets as lessee.
- SPV receives periodic rentals from the obligator.
- These are distributed among the investors *i.e.,* the sukuk holders.
- At maturity, or on a dissolution event, the SPV sells the assets back to the seller at a predetermined value. That value should be equal to any amounts still owed under the terms of the Ijara sukuk.

Ijara Sukuk in Practice

In December 2000, Kumpulan Guthrie Berhad (Guthrie) was granted a RM 1.5 billion (US$400 million) Al-Ijara Al-Muntahiyah Bit-Tamik by a consortium of banks. The original facility was raised to re-finance Guthrie's acquisition of a palm oil plantation in the Republic of Indonesia. The consortium was then invited to participate as the underwriter/primary subscriber of the Sukuk Transaction.

US$350 million sukuk Trust Certificates by Sarawak Corporate Sukuk Inc. (SCSI) Sarawak Economic Development Corporation (SEDC) raised financing amounting to US$350 million by way of issuance of series of trust certificates issued on the principle of Ijara sukuk. The certificates were issued with a maturity of 5 years and under the proposed structure, the proceeds will be used by the issuer to purchase certain assets from 1st Silicon (Malaysia) Sdn Bhd. Thereafter, the issuer will lease assets procured from 1st Silicon to SEDC for an agreed rental price for an agreed lease period of 5 years.

4. *Murabaha Sukuk*

In this case the issuer of the certificate is the seller of the Murabaha commodity, the subscribers are the buyers of that commodity, and the realised funds are the purchasing cost of the commodity. The certificate holders own the Murabaha commodity and are entitled to its final sale price upon the re-sale of the Commodity. The possibility of having legally acceptable Murabaha-based sukuk is only feasible in the primary market. The negotiability of these Sukuk or their trading at the secondary market is not permitted by shariah, as the certificates represent a debt owing from the subsequent buyer of the Commodity to the certificate-holders and such trading amounts to trading in debt on a deferred basis, which will result in riba.

Despite being debt instruments, the Murabaha Sukuk could be negotiable if they are the smaller part of a package or a portfolio, the larger part of which is constituted of negotiable instruments such as Mudaraba, Musharaka, or Ijara Sukuk. Murabaha sukuk are popular in Malaysian market due to a more liberal interpretation of fiqh by Malaysian jurists permitting sale of debt (bai-al-dayn) at a negotiated price.

Steps involved in the structure:

- A master agreement is signed between the SPV and the borrower.
- SPV issues sukuk to the investors and receive sukuk proceeds.
- SPV buys commodity on spot basis from the commodity supplier.
- SPV sells the commodity to the borrower at the spot price plus a profit margin, payable on installments over an agreed period of time
- The borrower sells the commodity to the Commodity buyer on spot basis.
- The investors receive the final sale price and profits.

Murabaha Sukuk in Practice

Arcapita Bank, a Bahrain-based investment firm has mandated Bayerische Hypo-und Vereinsbank AG ('HVB'), Standard Bank Plc ('SB') and West LB AG, London Branch ('WestLB') (together the 'Mandated Lead Arrangers'), to arrange a Five Year Multicurrency (US$, • and £) Murabaha-backed Sukuk. Sukuk will have a five-year bullet maturity and proposed pricing three month LIBOR + 175bps.

5. *Salam Sukuk*

Salam sukuk are certificates of equal value issued for the purpose of mobilising Salam capital so that the goods to be delivered on the basis of Salam come to the ownership of the certificate holders. The issuer of the certificates is a seller of the goods of Salam, the subscribers are the buyers of the goods, while the funds realised from subscription are the purchase price (Salam capital) of the goods. The holders of Salam certificates are the owners of the Salam goods and are entitled to the sale price of the certificates or the sale price of the Salam goods sold through a parallel Salam, if any.

Salam-based securities may be created and sold by an SPV under which the funds mobilised from investors are paid as an advance to the company SPV in return for a promise to deliver a commodity at a future date. SPV can also appoint an agent to market the promised quantity at the time of delivery perhaps at a higher price. The difference between the purchase price and the sale price is the profit to the SPV and hence to the holders of the Sukuk.

All standard shariah requirements that apply to Salam also apply to Salam sukuk, such as, full payment by the buyer at the time of effecting the sale, standardised nature of underlying asset, clear enumeration of quantity, quality, date and place of delivery of the asset and the like.

One of the Shariah conditions relating to Salam, as well as for creation of Salam sukuk, is the requirement that the purchased goods are not re-sold before actual possession at maturity. Such transactions amount to selling of debt. This constraint renders the Salam instrument illiquid and hence somewhat less attractive to investors. Thus, an investor will buy a Salam certificate if he expects prices of the underlying commodity to be higher on the maturity date.

Steps involved in the transaction:

- SPV signs an undertaking with an obligator to source both commodities and buyers. The obligator contracts to buy, on behalf of the end-Sukuk holders, the commodity and then to sell it for the profit of the Sukuk holders.
- Salam certificates are issued to investors and SPV receives Sukuk proceeds.
- The Salam proceeds are passed onto the obligator who sells commodity on forward basis
- SPV receives the commodities from the obligator.
- Obligator, on behalf of Sukuk holders, sells the commodities for a profit.
- Sukuk holders receive the commodity sale proceeds.

Salam Sukuk in Practice

Aluminum has been designated as the underlying asset of the Bahrain Government al Salam contract, where by it promises to sell aluminum to the buyer at a specified future date in return of a full price payment in advance. The

Bahrain Islamic Bank (BIB) has been nominated to represent the other banks wishing to participate in the Al Salam contract. BIB has been delegated to sign the contracts and all other necessary documents on behalf of the other banks in the syndicate. At the same time, the buyer appoints the Government of Bahrain as an agent to market the appropriate quantity at the time of delivery through its channels of distribution. The Government of Bahrain provides an additional undertaking to the representative (BIB) to market the aluminum at a price, which will provide a return to al Salam security holders equivalent to those available through other conventional short-term money market instruments.

6. *Istisna Sukuk*

Istisna sukuk are certificates that carry equal value and are issued with the aim of mobilising the funds required for producing products that are owned by the certificate holders. The issuer of these certificates is the manufacturer (supplier/seller), the subscribers are the buyers of the intended product, while the funds realised from subscription are the cost of the product. The certificate holders own the product and are entitled to the sale price of the certificates or the sale price of the product sold on the basis of a parallel Istisna, if any. Istisna Sukuk are quite useful for financing large infrastructure projects. The suitability of Istisna for financial intermediation is based on the permissibility for the contractor in Istisna to enter into a parallel Istisna contract with a subcontractor. Thus, a financial institution may undertake the construction of a facility for a deferred price, and sub contract the actual construction to a specialised firm. Shariah prohibits the sale of these debt certificates to a third party at any price other than their face value. Clearly such certificates cannot be traded in the secondary market.

Steps involved in the structure:

- SPV issues Sukuk certificates to raise funds for the project.
- Sukuk issue proceeds are used to pay the contractor/builder to build and deliver the future project.

- Title to assets is transferred to the SPV.
- Property/project is leased or sold to the end buyer. The end buyer pays monthly installments to the SPV.
- The returns are distributed among the Sukuk holders.

Istisna Sukuk in Practice

Tabreed's five-year global corporate Sukuk (on behalf of the National Central Cooling Company, UAE) provided a fixed coupon of 5.50 per cent. It is a combination of Ijara Istisna and Ijara Mawsufah fial dhimmah (or forward leasing contracts). The issue was launched to raise funds to retire some existing debt, which totals around US$136 million, as well as to finance expansion.

The Durrat Sukuk will finance the reclamation and infrastructure for the initial stage of a broader US$ 1 billion world class residential and leisure destination known as 'Durrat Al Bahrain', currently the Kingdom of Bahrain's largest residential development project. The return on the Sukuk is 125 basis points over 3 months LIBOR payable quarterly, with the Sukuk having an overall tenor of 5 years and an option for early redemption. The proceeds of the issue (cash) will be used by the Issuer to finance the reclamation of the land and the development of Base Infrastructure through multiple project finance (Istisna) agreements. As the works carried out under each Istisna are completed by the Contractor and delivered to the Issuer, the Issuer will give notice to the Project Company under the Master Ijara Agreement and will lease such Base Infrastructure on the basis of a lease to own transaction.

7. *Hybrid Sukuk*

Considering the fact that Sukuk issuance and trading are important means of investment and taking into account the various demands of investors, a more diversified Sukuk – hybrid or mixed asset Sukuk – emerged in the market. In a hybrid Sukuk, the underlying pool of assets can comprise of Istisna, Murabaha receivables as well as Ijara. Having a portfolio of assets comprising of different classes allows for a greater mobilisation of funds. However, as Murabaha and

Istisna contracts cannot be traded on secondary markets as securitised instruments at least 51 per cent of the pool in a hybrid Sukuk must comprise of Sukuk tradable in the market such as an Ijara Sukuk. Due to the fact the Murabaha and Istisna receivables are part of the pool, the return on these certificates can only be a pre-determined fixed rate of return.

Steps involved in the structure:

- Islamic finance originator transfers tangible assets as well as Murabaha deals to the SPV.
- SPV issues certificates of participation to the Sukuk holders and receive funds. The funds are used by the Islamic finance originator.
- Islamic finance originator purchase these assets from the SPV over an agreed period of time.
- Investors receive fixed payment of return on the assets.

Hybrid Sukuk in Practice

Islamic Development Bank issued the first hybrid Sukuk of assets comprising 65.8 per cent Sukuk al-Ijara, 30.73 per cent of Murabaha receivables and 3.4 per cent Sukuk al-Istisna. This issuance required the IDB's guarantee in order to secure a rating and international marketability. The $ 400 million Islamic Sukuk was issued by Solidarity Trust Services Limited (STSL), a special purpose company incorporated in Jersey Channel Islands. The Islamic Corporation for the Development of Private Sector (ICD) played an intermediary role by purchasing the asset from IDB and selling it to The Solidarity Trust Services Limited (STSL) at the consolidated net asset value.

Conclusion

The market for sukuk is now maturing and there is an increasing momentum in the wake of interest from issuers and investors. Sukuk have confirmed their viability as an alternative means to mobilise medium to long-term savings and investments from a huge investor base.

Different sukuk structures have been emerging over the years but most of the sukuk issuance to date have been ijara sukuk, since they are based on the undivided pro-rata ownership of the underlying leased asset, it is freely tradable at par, premium or discount. Tradability of the sukuk in the secondary market makes them more attractive. Although less common than Ijara sukuk, other types of sukuk are also playing significant role in emerging markets to help issuers and investors alike to participate in major projects, including airports, bridges, power plants etc. The sovereign sukuk issues, following Malaysia's lead, are enjoying widespread and positive acclaim among Islamic investors and global institutional investors alike.

Examples of Sukuk Issuances and their Structures

Standard and Poor's estimates that 20 per cent of those investors, with billions to invest, would now spontaneously choose an Islamic financial product over a conventional one with a similar risk-return profile.

That has led to the increased use of the Sukuk, especially in the Gulf countries and Malaysia. The Accounting and Auditing Organization for Islamic Financial Institutions (AAOIFI), defines Sukuks as "certificates of equal value representing after closing subscription, receipt of the value of the certificates and putting it to use as planned, common title to shares and rights in tangible assets, usufructs and services, or equity of a given project or equity of a special investment activity".

Introduced in varied structures and sizes, Sukuks worth $20 billion hit the market in 2006 and are expected to surpass $50 billion in 2007 as the companies seek to diversify their sources of financing. Although companies in Kuwait, Bahrain, Saudi Arabia and Qatar have all been actively using Sukuk financings over the years, Malaysia led the Sukuk issue market in 2006 with a share of about 60 per cent. That year also witnessed the first Sukuk that originated in the United States. The trends in 2007 clearly suggest that the United Arab Emirates, especially Dubai, have most likely taken over the lead.

Sukuk structures are being used for a variety of purposes and have evolved rapidly in response to the demands of issuers and investors. Sukuk issues have ranged from the simple sale and leaseback (Ijara) structures, such as the $1 billion Dubai Department of Civil Aviation Sukuk issued in November 2004, to the $2.53 billion trust finance Sukuk structure issued by Aldar Properties in March 2007, demonstrating the flexibility of Islamic finance principles.

Below are examples of some recent Sukuk issues that show and emphasise that Sukuk has matured into a diversified, internationally-acceptable instrument to raise corporate finance for acquisitions or working capital purposes, or to re-finance existing debt, or use in the transportation sector (especially in the shipping and aircraft sectors), real estate, construction and petrochemical projects in several countries.

German Sukuk (Saxony-Anhalt Sukuk)

In 2004, a •100 million Sukuk, structured as a Sukuk Al Ijara, was issued in the federal state of Saxony-Anhalt in Germany. The Federal Republic of Germany guarantees the debts of Saxony-Anhalt. The underlying transactions are a certain number of specified buildings owned by the Ministry of Finance. The master lease was sold for 100 years to a special purpose vehicle, incorporated in the Netherlands for tax reasons, which in turn rented it back for five years to the Ministry of Finance. The certificate holders receive a variable rent benchmarked to the EURIBOR over the rented period. The Sukuk is listed on the Luxembourg Stock Exchange. Incidentally, as of July 2007, the Saxony-Anhalt Sukuk remains the only sovereign Sukuk from a non-Islamic country to have tapped the market.

Sukuks by the Governments of Bahrain, Qatar and Malaysia

The Central Bank of Bahrain, on behalf of the Government of Bahrain, regularly issues Sukuk-Al-Ijara and Sukuk Al-Salam to finance various infrastructure projects in Bahrain. Malaysia's Global Sukuk, launched in June 2002, was similarly backed by an Ijara lease on a single piece of government property. The money raised by the Government of Qatar through the $700 million Qatar Global Sukuk is being used partly to finance the construction of the Hamad Medical City.

First Airlines Sukuk – Emirates Airlines Sukuk

The first Sukuk issued by Dubai's national airlines, Emirates, closed in July 2005. At $550 million, this was the single largest corporate Sukuk issuance at that time. The Sukuk has a seven-year tenor and is structured as a Musharaka. The proceeds of the issue, which is listed on the Luxembourg Stock Exchange, will be used to finance the new Emirates Engineering Centre and their headquarters building in Dubai.

First Ship Finance Sukuk – MT Venus Glory Sukuk/ Al Safeena Sukuk

In 2005, ABC International Bank jointly with Abu Dhabi Commercial Bank arranged, structured and jointly underwrote a pioneering Islamic ship finance transaction through the issuance of a $26 million Al-Safeena Ijara Sukuk. At that time, Al-Safeena Sukuk was the first issue that combined Islamic equity with conventional debt for the same asset, which in this case was VLCC (called 'Venus Glory'), owned by Pacific Star (Pac Star) International Holding Corporation, which in turn is owned by Saudi Aramco, the world's largest oil exporting company.

Dubai Civil Aviation Authority Sukuk

The Dubai Civil Aviation Authority, a quasi-sovereign entity, broke the mould in 2004 by going down the Sukuk route instead of plain vanilla finance, by issuing a $1 billion Sukuk, the world's largest single Sukuk issuance in terms of size at that time by any issuer. The proceeds were used to finance the building of a new international terminal and for the expansion of existing engineering and other infrastructure. The Musharaka was set up to develop a new engineering centre and a new headquarters building on land situated near Dubai's airport that will ultimately be leased to Emirates. Profit, in the form of lease returns, generated from the Musharaka will be used to pay the periodic distribution on the trust certificates.

Bahrain Financial Harbour – Al Marfa'a Al Mali Sukuk

The Istisna'a-Ijara Sukuk, known as the Al Marfa'a Al Mali Sukuk, has been structured by the Liquidity Management Centre in accordance and in compliance with the principles of Islamic Shari'a. The Sukuk has a five-year term maturing in 2010 offering a quarterly profit distribution with the proceeds used to finance the development and construction of the Financial Centre which represents the first phase of the Bahrain Financial Harbour project comprising the Dual Towers, the Financial Mall and the Harbour House.

Dubai World Sukuk

In 2006, Dubai property developer Nakheel Group, developer of three palm-frond shaped islands off Dubai's coast, sold the world's largest Islamic bond after increasing its size by more than 40 per cent to $3.52 billion to meet demand. Nakheel will use cash from its Sukuk to fund projects in Dubai, which is leading a surge in Gulf Arab investment in construction and real-estate developments. The Sukuk has been listed on the Dubai International Financial Exchange.

DP World Sukuk

In 2007, global marine terminal operator DP World priced a $1.75 billion conventional bond and a $1.5 billion Sukuk. It is the first issuer to list both conventional and Islamic debt securities on the Dubai International Financial Exchange.

The $1.5 billion, 10-year Sukuk attracted demand globally, including from the United States. This was the first time U.S., investors had the opportunity to subscribe to a UAE corporate rated Sukuk. DP World's Sukuk is ground breaking and innovative because it is partly convertible to shares in the event the ports group lists through an initial public offering, thus becoming the first convertible instrument in the Islamic finance market. The issue is part of a large financing package being arranged for general corporate activities, ongoing business development needs, and expansion plans, including the financing of the purchase of the British rival P and O.

East Cameron Gas Sukuk

The first and only Sukuk to have originated from the United States tapped the market in 2006. The unique feature of the East Cameron Gas Sukuk was that it was the first ever Shariah compliant gas backed securitisation and was the first-ever Islamic securitisation rated by Standard and Poor's. The $165.7 million Sukuk originated from Houston based East Cameron Partners, whose reserves are located in the shallow waters off the shores of the State of Louisana. The Sukuk was structured as a Musharaka structure in terms of the management of the assets and then a funding agreement between the issuer and the purchaser.

The initiatives taken by the governments of the UAE, Bahrain, Malaysia and the United Kingdom, to name a few, have acted as a catalyst for the evolution and growth of the Sukuk market and the development of Islamic Finance as a whole. The regulatory bodies within such countries have been actively introducing rules and regulations pertaining to the issuing and offering of Sukuks, which we hope in time will help provide standardisation, resulting in the maturation of the field.

From the financing structures focused mainly on plain vanilla type commodity-trading murabaha transactions to the complex structures involved in the Sukuks, Islamic finance has come a long way and Sukuks have emerged as high profile financial instruments. With top international banks, financial institutions, law firms and other financial services providers scampering for a piece of the cake in the Middle East, Islamic banking and finance has grown into a full-fledged practice area of its own. With a catalogue of successful issues worth billions of dollars reflecting the huge appetite for Sukuks, there are all signs pointing towards the long-term success and growth of Sukuks.

AAOIFI Shari'ah Resolutions: Issues on Sukuk

The Shari'ah Board of the Accounting and Auditing Organization for Islamic Financial Institutions (AAOIFI), in view of the increased use of sukuk worldwide, the public interest in them, and the observations and questions raised about them, studied the subject of the issuance of sukuk in three sessions; first, in al-Madinah al-Munawwarah, on 12 Jumada al-Akhirah 1428 AH (27 June 2007), second, in Makkah al-Mukarramah, on 26 Sh'aban 1428 AH (8 September 2007), and third, in the Kingdom of Bahrain on 7 and 8 Safar 1429AH (13 and 14 February 2008).

Following the meeting of the working group, appointed by the Board, which met in Bahrain, on 6 Muharram 1429AH (15 January 2007), which was also attended by a significant number of representatives from various Islamic banks and financial institutions, the working group presented its report to the Shari'ah Board.

After taking into consideration the deliberations in these meetings and reviewing the papers and studies presented therein, the Shari'ah Board – while re-affirming the rules provided in the AAOIFI Shari'ah Standards concerning Sukuk – advises Islamic financial institutions and Shari'ah Supervisory Boards to adhere to the following matters when issuing sukuk:

First, Sukuk, to be tradable, must be owned by the sukuk holders, with all the rights and obligations of ownership, in real assets, whether tangible, usufructs or services, capable of being owned and sold legally, as well as in accordance with the rules of the Shari'ah, in accordance with Articles (2) and (5/1/2) of the AAOIFI Shari'ah Standard (17) on Investment Sukuk. The Manager issuing the sukuk must certify the transfer of ownership of such assets in its (sukuk) books, and must not keep them as his own assets.

Second, Sukuk, to be tradable, must not represent receivables or debts, except in the case of a trading or financial entity selling all its assets, or a portfolio with a standing financial obligation, in which some debts, incidental to physical assets or usufruct, were included unintentionally, in accordance with the guidelines mentioned in AAOIFI Shari'ah Standard (21) on Financial Papers.

Third, It is not permissible for the Manager of sukuk, whether the manager acts as the mudharib (investment manager), or sharik (partner), or wakil (agent) for investment, to undertake to offer loans to sukuk holders, when actual earnings fall short of expected earnings. It is permissible, however, to establish a reserve account for the purpose of covering such shortfalls to the extent possible, provided the same is mentioned in the prospectus. It is not objectionable to distribute expected earnings, on account, in accordance with Article (8/8)3 of the AAOIFI Shari'ah Standard (13) on Mudaraba, or to obtain project financing on account of the sukuk holders.

Fourth, It is not permissible for the mudharib (investment manager), sharik (partner), or wakil (agent) to undertake {now} to re-purchase the assets from sukuk holders or from one who holds them, for its nominal value, when the sukuk are extinguished, at the end of its maturity. It is, however, permissible to undertake the purchase on the basis of the net value of assets, its market value, fair value or a price to be agreed, at the time of their actual purchase, in accordance with Article (3/1/6/2) of AAOIFI Shari'ah Standard (12) on Sharikah (Musharaka) and Modern Corporations, and Articles (2/2/1) and (2/2/2) of the AAOIFI Shari'ah Standard (5) on Guarantees. It is known that a sukuk manager is a guarantor of the capital, at its nominal value, in case of his negligent acts or omissions or his non-compliance with the investor's conditions, whether the manager is a mudharib (investment manager), sharik (partner) or wakil (agent) for investments.

In case the assets of sukuk of al-musharaka, mudharabah, or wakalah for investment are of lesser value than the leased assets of 'Lease to Own' contracts (Ijarah Muntahia Bittamleek), then it is permissible for the sukuk manager to undertake to purchase those assets – at the time the sukuk are extinguished – for the remaining rental value of the remaining assets; since it actually represents its net value.

Fifth, It is permissible for a lessee in a sukuk al-ijarah to undertake to purchase the leased assets when the sukuk are extinguished for its nominal value, provided he {lessee} is not also a partner, mudharib or investment agent.

Sixth, Shari'ah Supervisory Boards should not limit their role to the issuance of fatwa on the permissibility of the structure of sukuk. All relevant contracts and documents related to the actual transaction must be carefully reviewed {by them}, and then they should oversee the actual means of implementation, and then make sure that the operation complies, at every stage, with Shari'ah guidelines and requirements, as specified in the Shari'ah Standards. The investment of sukuk proceeds and the conversion of the proceeds into assets, using one of the Shari'ah-compliant methods of investments, must conform to Article (5/1/8/5) of the AAOIFI Shari'ah Standard (17).

Furthermore, the Shari'ah Board advises Islamic financial institutions to decrease their involvements in debt-related operations and to increase true partnerships based on profit and loss sharing, in order to achieve the objectives of the Shari'ah.

CHAPTER

8

Venture Capital

Venture capital (also known as VC or Venture) is a type of private equity capital typically provided to early-stage, high-potential, growth companies in the interest of generating a return through an eventual realisation event such as an IPO or trade sale of the company. Venture capital investments are generally made as cash in exchange for shares in the invested company. It is typical for venture capital investors to identify and back companies in high technology industries such as biotechnology and ICT.

Venture capital typically comes from institutional investors and high net worth individuals and is pooled together by dedicated investment firms.

Venture capital firms typically comprise small teams with technology backgrounds (scientists, researchers) or those with business training or deep industry experience. VC has a reputation of being a particularly impenetrable career path, employing only those who bring expert value.

A core skill within VC is the ability to identify novel technologies that have the potential to generate high commercial returns at an early stage. By definition, VCs also take a role in managing entrepreneurial companies at an early stage, thus adding skills as well as capital (thereby differentiating VC from buy out private equity which typically invest in companies with proven revenue), and thereby potentially realising much higher rates of returns.

A venture capitalist (also known as a VC) is a person or investment firm that makes venture investments, and these venture capitalists are expected to bring managerial and technical expertise as well as capital to their investments. A venture capital fund refers to a pooled investment vehicle (often an LP or LLC) that primarily invests the financial capital of third-party investors in enterprises that are too risky for the standard capital markets or bank loans.

Venture capital is also associated with job creation, the knowledge economy and used as a proxy measure of innovation within an economic sector or geography.

Venture capital is most attractive for new companies with limited operating history that are too small to raise capital in the public markets and are too immature to secure a bank loan or complete a debt offering. In exchange for the high risk that venture capitalists assume by investing in smaller and less mature companies, venture capitalists usually get significant control over company decisions, in addition to a significant portion of the company's ownership (and consequently value).

Young companies wishing to raise venture capital require a combination of extremely rare yet sought after qualities, such as innovative technology, potential for rapid growth, well thought through business model and impressive management team. VCs typically reject 98 per cent of opportunities presented to them, reflecting the rarity of this combination.

History

With few exceptions, private equity in the first half of the 20th century was the domain of wealthy individuals and families. The Vanderbilts, Whitneys, Rockefellers and Warburgs were notable investors in private companies in the first half of the century. In 1938, Laurance S. Rockefeller helped finance the creation of both Eastern Air Lines and Douglas Aircraft and the Rockefeller family had vast holdings in a variety of companies. Eric M. Warburg founded E.M. Warburg and Co., in 1938, which would ultimately become Warburg Pincus, with investments in both leveraged buyouts and venture capital.

Origins of Modern Private Equity

Before World War II, venture capital investments (originally known as 'development capital') were primarily the domain of wealthy individuals and families. It was not until after World War II that what is considered today to be true private equity investments began to emerge marked by the founding of the first two venture capital firms in 1946: American Research and Development Corporation. (ARDC) and J.H. Whitney and Company.

ARDC was founded by Georges Doriot, the 'father of venture capitalism' (former dean of Harvard Business School), with Ralph Flanders and Karl Compton (former president of MIT), to encourage private sector investments in businesses run by soldiers who were returning from World War II. ARDC's significance was primarily that it was the first institutional private equity investment firm that raised capital from sources other than wealthy families although it had several notable investment successes as well. ARDC is credited with the first major venture capital success story when its 1957 investment of $70,000 in Digital Equipment Corporation (DEC) would be valued at over $355 million after the company's initial public offering in 1968 (representing a return of over 1200 times on its investment and an annualized rate of return of 101%). Former employees of ARDC went on and established several prominent venture capital firms including Greylock Partners (founded in 1965 by Charlie Waite and Bill Elfers) and Morgan, Holland Ventures, the predecessor of Flagship Ventures (founded in 1982 by James Morgan). ARDC continued investing until 1971 with the retirement of Doriot. In 1972, Doriot merged ARDC with Textron after having invested in over 150 companies.

J.H. Whitney and Company was founded by John Hay Whitney and his partner Benno Schmidt. Whitney had been investing since the 1930s, founding Pioneer Pictures in 1933 and acquiring a 15 per cent interest in Technicolor Corporation with his cousin Cornelius Vanderbilt Whitney. By far Whitney's most famous investment was in Florida Foods Corporation. The company developed an innovative method for delivering nutrition to American soldiers, which later came to be known as Minute Maid orange juice and was sold to The Coca-Cola Company in 1960. J.H. Whitney and Company continues to make investments in leveraged buyout transactions and raised $750 million for its sixth institutional private equity fund in 2005.

Early Venture Capital and the Growth of Silicon Valley

One of the first steps toward a professionally-managed venture capital industry was the passage of the Small Business Investment Act of 1958. The 1958 Act officially allowed the U.S. Small Business Administration (SBA) to license private 'Small Business Investment Companies' (SBICs) to help the financing and management of the small entrepreneurial businesses in the United States.

During the 1960s and 1970s, venture capital firms focused their investment activity primarily on starting and expanding companies. More often than not, these companies were exploiting breakthroughs in electronic, medical or data-processing technology. As a result, venture capital came to be almost synonymous with technology finance.

It is commonly noted that the first venture-backed startup is Fairchild Semiconductor (which produced the first commercially practical integrated circuit), funded in 1959 by what would later become Venrock Associates. Venrock was founded in 1969 by Laurance S. Rockefeller, the fourth of John D. Rockefeller's six children as a way to allow other Rockefeller children to develop exposure to venture capital investments.

It was also in the 1960s that the common form of private equity fund, still in use today, emerged. Private equity firms organized limited partnerships to hold investments in which the investment professionals served as general partner and the investors, who were passive limited partners, put up the capital. The compensation structure, still in use today, also emerged with limited partners paying an annual management fee of 1-2 per cent and a carried interest typically representing up to 20 per cent of the profits of the partnership.

The growth of the venture capital industry was fueled by the emergence of the independent investment firms on Sand Hill Road, beginning with Kleiner, Perkins, Caufield and Byers and Sequoia Capital in 1972. Located, in Menlo Park, CA, Kleiner Perkins, Sequoia and later venture capital firms would have access to the burgeoning technology industries in the area. By the early 1970s, there were many semiconductor companies based in the Santa Clara Valley as well as early computer firms using their devices and programming and service companies. Throughout the 1970s, a group of private equity firms, focused primarily on venture capital investments, would be founded that would become the model for later leveraged buyout and venture capital investment firms. In 1973, with the number of new venture capital firms increasing, leading venture capitalists formed the National Venture Capital Association (NVCA). The NVCA was to serve as the industry trade group for the venture capital industry. Venture capital firms suffered a temporary downturn in 1974, when the stock market crashed and investors were naturally wary of this new kind of investment fund.

It was not until 1978 that venture capital experienced its first major fundraising year, as the industry raised approximately $750 million. With the passage of the Employee Retirement Income Security Act (ERISA) in 1974, corporate pension funds were prohibited from holding certain risky investments including many investments in privately held companies. In 1978, the US Labour Department relaxed certain of the ERISA restrictions, under the 'prudent man rule', thus allowing corporate pension funds to invest in the asset class and providing a major source of capital available to venture capitalists.

Venture Capital in the 1980s

The public successes of the venture capital industry in the 1970s and early 1980s (*e.g.*, Digital Equipment Corporation, Apple Inc., Genentech) gave rise to a major proliferation of venture capital investment firms. From just a few dozen firms at the start of the decade, there were over 650 firms by the end of the 1980s, each searching for the next major 'home run'. While the number of firms multiplied, the capital managed by these firms increased by only 11 per cent from $28 billion to $31 billion over the course of the decade.

The growth the industry was hampered by sharply declining returns and certain venture firms began posting losses for the first time. In addition to the increased competition among firms, several other factors impacted returns. The market for initial public offerings cooled in the mid-1980s before collapsing after the stock market crash in 1987 and foreign corporations, particularly from Japan and Korea, flooded early stage companies with capital.

In response to the changing conditions, corporations that had sponsored in-house venture investment arms, including General Electric and Paine Webber either sold off or closed these venture capital units. Additionally, venture capital units within Chemical Bank and Continental Illinois National Bank, among others, began shifting their focus from funding early stage companies toward investments in more mature companies. Even industry founders J.H. Whitney and Company and Warburg Pincus began to transition toward leveraged buyouts and growth capital investments.

The Venture Capital Boom and the Internet Bubble (1995 to 2000)

By the end of the 1980s, venture capital returns were relatively low, particularly in comparison with their emerging leveraged buyout cousins, due in part to the competition for hot startups, excess supply of IPOs and the inexperience of many venture capital fund managers. Growth in the venture capital industry remained limited throughout the 1980s and the first half of the 1990s increasing from $3 billion in 1983 to just over $4 billion more than a decade later in 1994.

After a shakeout of venture capital managers, the more successful firms retrenched, focusing increasingly on improving operations at their portfolio companies rather than continuously making new investments. Results would begin to turn very attractive, successful and would ultimately generate the venture capital boom of the 1990s. Former Wharton Professor Andrew Metrick refers to these first 15 years of the modern venture capital industry beginning in 1980 as the 'pre-boom period' in anticipation of the boom that would begin in 1995 and last through the bursting of the Internet bubble in 2000.

The late 1990s were a boom time for the venture capital, as firms on Sand Hill Road in Menlo Park and Silicon Valley benefited from a huge surge of interest in the nascent Internet and other computer technologies. Initial public offerings of stock for technology and other growth companies were in abundance and venture firms were reaping large returns.

The Bursting of the Internet Bubble and the Private Equity Crash (2000-03)

The Nasdaq crash and technology slump that started in March 2000 shook virtually the entire venture capital industry as valuations for startup technology companies collapsed. Over the next two years, many venture firms had been forced to write-off their large proportions of their investments and many funds were significantly 'under water' (the values of the fund's investments were below the amount of capital invested). Venture capital investors sought to reduce size of commitments they had made to venture capital funds and in numerous instances, investors sought to unload existing commitments for cents on the dollar in the secondary market. By mid-2003, the venture capital industry had shriveled to about half its 2001 capacity. Nevertheless, Pricewaterhouse Coopers' Money Tree Survey shows that total venture capital investments held steady at 2003 levels through the second quarter of 2005.

Although the post-boom years represent just a small fraction of the peak levels of venture investment reached in 2000, they still represent an increase over the levels of investment from 1980 through 1995. As a percentage of GDP, venture investment was 0.058 per cent per cent in 1994, peaked at 1.087 per cent (nearly 19x the 1994 level) in 2000 and ranged from 0.164 per cent to 0.182 per cent in 2003 and 2004. The revival of an Internet-driven environment in 2004 through 2007 helped to revive the venture capital environment. However, as a percentage of the overall private equity market, venture capital has still not reached its mid-1990s level, let alone its peak in 2000.

Venture capital funds, which were responsible for much of the fundraising volume in 2000 (the height of the dot-com bubble), raised only $25.1 billion in 2006, a 2 per cent per cent decline from 2005 and a significant decline from its peak.

Structure of Venture Capital Firms

Venture capital firms are typically structured as partnerships, the general partners of which serve as the managers of the firm and will serve as investment advisors to the venture capital funds raised. Venture capital firms in the United States may also be structured as limited liability companies, in which case the firm's managers are known as managing members. Investors in venture capital funds are known as limited partners. This constituency comprises both high net worth individuals and institutions with large amounts of available capital, such as state and private pension funds, university financial endowments, foundations, insurance companies, and pooled investment vehicles, called fund of funds or mutual funds.

Types of Venture Capital Firms

Depending on your type business, the venture capital firm you approach will differ. For instance, if you're an internet [startup company], funding requests from a more manufacturing-focused firm will not be effective. Doing some initial research on which firms to approach will save time and effort. When approaching a VC firm, consider their portfolio:

- *Business Cycle*: Do they invest in budding or established businesses?

- *Industry:* What is their industry focus?
- *Investment*: Is their typical investment sufficient for your needs?
- *Location*: Are they regional, national or international?
- *Return:* What is their expected return on investment?
- *Involvement:* What is their involvement level?

Targeting specific types of firms will yield the best results when seeking VC financing. Wikipedia has a list of venture capital firms that can help you in your initial exploration. The National Venture Capital Association segments dozens of VC firms into ways that might assist you in your search. It is important to note that many VC firms have diverse portfolios with a range of clients. If this is the case, finding gaps in their portfolio is one strategy that might succeed.

Roles within Venture Capital Firms

Within the venture capital industry, the general partners and other investment professionals of the venture capital firm are often referred to as 'venture capitalists' or 'VCs'. Typical career backgrounds vary, but broadly speaking venture capitalists come from either an operational or a finance background. Venture capitalists with an operational background tend to be former founders or executives of companies similar to those which the partnership finances or will have served as management consultants. Venture capitalists with finance backgrounds tend to have investment banking or other corporate finance experience.

Although the titles are not entirely uniform from firm to firm, other positions at venture capital firms include:

- *Venture partners*: Venture partners are expected to source potential investment opportunities ('bring in deals') and typically are compensated only for those deals with which they are involved.
- *Entrepreneur-in-residence (EIR)*: EIRs are experts in a particular domain and perform due diligence on potential deals. EIRs are engaged by venture capital firms temporarily (six to 18 months) and are expected to

develop and pitch startup ideas to their host firm (although neither party is bound to work with each other). Some EIR's move on to executive positions within a portfolio company.

- *Principal*: This is a mid-level investment professional position, and often considered a 'partner-track' position. Principals will have been promoted from a senior associate position or who have commensurate experience in another field such as investment banking or management consulting.
- *Associate*: This is typically the most junior apprentice position within a venture capital firm. After a few successful years, an associate may move up to the 'senior associate' position and potentially principal and beyond. Associates will often have worked for 1-2 years in another field such as investment banking or management consulting.

Structure of the Funds

Most venture capital funds have a fixed life of 10 years, with the possibility of a few years of extensions to allow for private companies still seeking liquidity. The investing cycle for most funds is generally three to five years, after which the focus is managing and making follow-on investments in an existing portfolio. This model was pioneered by successful funds in Silicon Valley through the 1980s to invest in technological trends broadly but only during their period of ascendance, and to cut exposure to management and marketing risks of any individual firm or its product.

In such a fund, the investors have a fixed commitment to the fund that is initially unfunded and subsequently 'called down' by the venture capital fund over time as the fund makes its investments. There are substantial penalties for a Limited Partner (or investor) that fails to participate in a capital call.

It can take anywhere from a month or so to several years for venture capitalists to raise money from limited partners for their fund. At the time when all of the money has been raised, the fund is said to be closed and the 10 year lifetime begins. Some funds have partial closes when one half (or some other amount) of the fund has been raised. 'Vintage year' generally refers to the year in which the fund was closed and may serve as a means to stratify VC funds for comparison. This free database of venture capital funds shows the difference between a venture capital fund management company and the venture capital funds managed by them.

Compensation

Venture capitalists are compensated through a combination of management fees and carried interest (often referred to as a 'two and 20' arrangement:

- *Management fees*: An annual payment made by the investors in the fund to the fund's manager to pay for the private equity firm's investment operations. In a typical venture capital fund, the general partners receive an annual management fee equal to up to 2 per cent of the committed capital.
- *Carried interest*: A share of the profits of the fund (typically 20%), paid to the private equity fund's management company as a performance incentive. The remaining 80 per cent of the profits are paid to the fund's investors Strong Limited Partner interest in top-tier venture firms has led to a general trend toward terms more favorable to the venture partnership, and certain groups are able to command carried interest of 25-30 per cent on their funds.

Because a fund may run out of capital prior to the end of its life, larger venture capital firms usually have several overlapping funds at the same time; this lets the larger firm keep specialists in all stages of the development of firms almost constantly engaged. Smaller firms tend to thrive or fail with their initial industry contacts; by the time the fund cashes out, an entirely-new generation of technologies and people is ascending, whom the general partners may not know well, and so it is prudent to reassess and shift industries or personnel rather than attempt to simply invest more in the industry or people the partners already know.

Venture Capital Funding

Venture capitalists are typically very selective in deciding what to invest in; as a rule of thumb, a fund may invest in one in four hundred opportunities presented to it. Funds are most interested in ventures with exceptionally high growth potential, as only such opportunities are likely capable of providing the financial returns and successful exit event within the required timeframe (typically 3-7 years) that venture capitalists expect.

Because investments are illiquid and require 3-7 years to harvest, venture capitalists are expected to carry out detailed due diligence prior to investment. Venture capitalists also are expected to nurture the companies in which they invest, in order to increase the likelihood of reaching a IPO stage when valuations are favourable. Venture capitalists typically assist at four stages in the company's development:

1. Idea generation.
2. Start-up.
3. Ramp up.
4. Exit.

There are typically six stages of financing offered in Venture Capital, that roughly correspond to these stages of a company's development.

(i) *Seed Money*: Low level financing needed to prove a new idea (Often provided by 'angel investors').

(ii) *Start-up*: Early stage firms that need funding for expenses associated with marketing and product development.

(iii) *First-Round*: Early sales and manufacturing funds.

(iv) *Second-Round*: Working capital for early stage companies that are selling product, but not yet turning a profit.

(v) *Third-Round*: Also called Mezzanine financing, this is expansion money for a newly profitable company.

(vi) *Fourth-Round*: Also called bridge financing, 4th round is intended to finance the 'going public' process.

Because there are no public exchanges listing their securities, private companies meet venture capital firms and other private equity investors in several ways, including warm referrals from the investors' trusted sources and other business contacts; investor conferences and symposia; and summits where companies pitch directly to investor groups in face-to-face meetings, including a variant know as 'Speed Venturing', which is akin to speed-dating for capital, where the investor decides within 10 minutes whether she/he wants a follow-up meeting.

This need for high returns makes venture funding an expensive capital source for companies, and most suitable for businesses having large up-front capital requirements which cannot be financed by cheaper alternatives such as debt. That is most commonly the case for intangible assets such as software, and other intellectual property, whose value is unproven. In turn this explains why venture capital is most prevalent in the fast-growing technology and life sciences or biotechnology fields.

If a company does have the qualities venture capitalists seek including a solid business plan, a good management team, investment and passion from the founders, a good potential to exit the investment before the end of their funding cycle, and target minimum returns in excess of 40 per cent per year, it will find it easier to raise venture capital.

Main Alternatives to Venture Capital

Because of the strict requirements venture capitalists have for potential investments, many entrepreneurs seek initial funding from angel investors, who may be more willing to invest in highly speculative opportunities, or may have a prior relationship with the entrepreneur.

Furthermore, many venture capital firms will only seriously evaluate an investment in a start-up otherwise unknown to them if the company can prove at least some of its claims about the technology and/or market potential for its product or services. To achieve this, or even just to avoid the dilutive effects of receiving funding before such claims are proven, many start-ups seek to self-finance until they reach a point where they can credibly approach outside capital providers such as venture capitalists or angel investors. This practice is called 'bootstrapping'.

There has been some debate since the dot com boom that a 'funding gap' has developed between the friends and family investments typically in the $0 to $250,000 range and the amounts that most Venture Capital Funds prefer to invest between $1 to $2M. This funding gap may be accentuated by the fact that some successful Venture Capital funds have been drawn to raise ever-larger funds, requiring them to search for correspondingly larger investment opportunities. This 'gap' is often filled by angel investors as well as equity investment companies who specialise in investments in startups from the range of $250,000 to $1M. The National Venture Capital association estimates that the latter now invest more than $30 billion a year in the USA in contrast to the $20 billion a year invested by organized Venture Capital funds.

In industries where assets can be securitised effectively because they reliably generate future revenue streams or have a good potential for resale in case of foreclosure, businesses may more cheaply be able to raise debt to finance their growth. Good examples would include asset-intensive extractive industries such as mining, or manufacturing industries. Offshore funding is provided via specialist venture capital trusts which seek to utilise securitisation in structuring hybrid multi market transactions via an SPV (special purpose vehicle): a corporate entity that is designed solely for the purpose of the financing.

In addition to traditional venture capital and angel networks, groups have emerged which allow groups of small investors or entrepreneurs themselves to compete in a privatised business plan competition where the group itself serves as the investor through a democratic process.

The Establishment of the VC Sector in the Islamic World

The introduction of the venture capital industry into a country encourages and supports entrepreneurs, creates jobs and tax revenue and makes possible the development of high technology. This being the case, no government would want to oppose it and there is no reason why Islamic countries should not benefit from it as much as the West has done.

Equity investments in permissible sectors are allowed in Islam (Siddiqi, 1985; Chapra, 1992), as are investments in companies having a zero conventional debt capital structure (Khan, 1989; Khan, 1995). The provision of equity-based capital for Small and Medium Enterprises (SMEs) also accords with the Islamic desire for wider economic development and a more equal distribution of wealth. Islamic banks have a special role to play in the establishment of the VC sector in Islamic countries. This is because the structure of the two organizations is basically the same. They are both involved in profit-and-loss-sharing (PLS) and have a common history.

Their history started with the Islamic mudarabah a form of partnership used even before Islam by Arab traders. Later the mudarabah was formalized and embodied in the Shari'ah law by the Muslim jurists. As Islamic culture spread across the world, the mudarabah went with it and continued to be used by Islamic businessmen until the 19th century. In about the 1970s, a kind of quantum leap happened and the concept of the modern Islamic bank emerged from these roots.

But there was another branch in this history. In the 10th century, the Italians took up the mudarabah and it spread through Europe. But while in Islam this partnership form remained undeveloped, in Europe, ever-increasing numbers of entrepreneurs were financed by them, so that the organizations became larger and larger. They became, in effect, what we now call VC companies.

So Islamic banks and VC companies have these common roots and that is why they are structurally similar. The similarities are briefly discussed below. The first level can be said to be the collection of funds. In Islamic banks, the investment account holders are people who participate in the bank's investments in order to share in the resulting profits under mudarabah, This is called profit-and-loss sharing (PLS) and the profits are shared according to an agreed ratio. In Turkey, for example, the ratio used to be 20/80, that is, the bank retains 20 per cent of the net profits and 80 per cent is distributed to the account holders.

In the VC sector, also, those who invest are taking part in a profit-sharing process. A ratio similar to that of the banks is used. On the second level, too, both Islamic banks and VC companies play the same role, that of mudarib or agent. Acting as an agent for their investors, they invest the investors' funds in a multitude of entrepreneurial companies and pass a proportion of the profits back to the investors, along with capital and gain where appropriate.

It may be argued that conventional Western banks play essentially the same role of agent between their depositors and the businesses they invest in. That is true, but there is a difference, which has important implications for the depositors. Instead of sharing in the profit or loss of the companies they invest in, conventional banks charge these companies a fixed rate of interest and give their depositors also a fixed, but lower, rate of interest. Making their profits from the difference between the two levels of interest, the banks are not participating in any real sense in the fortunes of the businesses they invest in. Nor are their depositors. Indeed, it is as though the bank had erected a wall between the two.

The similarity between Islamic banks and VC companies is closest when they use these PLS partnerships (either mudarabah or musharakah) with businesses. But the Islamic banks also use other forms of financing such as murabaha (renting equipment on a cost-plus basis) and there they differ from VC companies.

In other words, the similarity between Islamic banks and VC companies lies in the fact that they have the same philosophy of financing, that of sharing in the profit and loss of their investments and passing the results on to their depositors. For this reason, they use the same criteria in evaluating projects to invest in, namely, the ability of the entrepreneur and the profit potential of his project. As against this, conventional banks use the criteria of past performance, balance sheets and the credit-worthiness of the entrepreneur.

In case of loss, the Islamic banks have the same attitude as VC companies in that the capital loss is borne by the lender, the entrepreneur losing only to the extent that his labour has been lost.

Unfortunately, in practice, Islamic banks, in order to compete in fund mobilising with the West, have tended to show a preference for murabaha (cost-plus) financing, which is, of course, less risky than PLS. In order to introduce VC into Islamic countries, therefore, an effort will have to be made to persuade the Islamic banks to change their investment policies towards having more PLS contracts.

These are several reasons why Islamic banks tend to be reluctant to resort to PLS. *First*, the senior people now in Islamic banks mostly learned their trade in conventional banks and so tended to use those Islamic instruments which were nearest to the ones they were familiar with. Since risk minimization is one of the basic principles of conventional banks, the more risky PLS partnerships, particularly the mudaraba, where no money is contributed by the entrepreneur, were avoided.

Secondly, Islamic banks found themselves in fierce competition with conventional banks and felt that they could only attract funds by paying their depositors a profit share commensurate with the rate of interest paid by conventional banks. This was another reason for avoiding the more risky PLS investments.

Thirdly, in an economic environment dominated by inflation as well as high rates of interest, the Islamic banks did not want to venture into the long-investments required by PLS, but felt forced to design their portfolios on a short-term basis.

Fourthly, PLS involves close and continuing contact with the entrepreneurs financed and involvement in their problems, a situation the Islamic banks do not usually have the time or resources to cope with.

For all these reasons, conditions must change before a VC sector can be established in Islamic countries. To change them, a comprehensive reform package must be designed. Let us now look at what such a reform package must contain.

Models and Acceptable Structures for Islamic Venture Capital

Theoretical Models and Acceptable Structures

The basic theoretical model of an Islamic bank, according to Iqbal and Molyneux (2005), was developed on the lines of the Two-Tier Mudarabah (TTM) model. The rate of interest brings the asset and liability sides of conventional banking into equilibrium, whereas mudarabah is the primary profit and loss sharing (PLS) vehicle of asset and liability creation in Islamic banking. The bank is positioned between surplus groups (investors/depositors) and deficit groups (borrowers/ beneficiaries).

The TTM is an equity-based structure. On the liability side, the Islamic bank is assumed to play the role of Mudarib for the suppliers of capital (Rabb al-mals), while on the asset side it acts as the equity financier (Rahb al-ma!) for entrepreneurs (Miidaribs). The bank's return is therefore determined by a share of the profits on both sides of the TTM; banks share profits with their depositors and also with their beneficiaries. If a business venture fails, the capital provider (bank) loses its capital and labour provider (entrepreneur) loses his/her time and efforts.

Another prominent form of Islamic finance is musharakah; in this equity-based structure, two or more partners with a given amount of capital come together in a business venture. They share profit in a predetermined ratio (Siddiqi, 1985). Entrepreneurs are permitted to contribute to the total funds requirement, but it is only in musharakah that the partners may incur a financial loss, strictly in proportion to their capital contribution.

Both mudarabah and musharakah are equity-based, profit sharing structures, although there are some key differences between the two forms of funding. The main difference is that the entrepreneur offers no capital contribution in mudarabah, and therefore she/he is not liable to incur any financial loss apart from losing his/her effort (cost of labour) if the venture fails. Moreover, the bank is not authorised to participate in the management of a mudarabah project hence this form of financing carries a greater degree of risk. In a project financed by musharakah, the bank has right to participate in management unless it deliberately waives the right to do so. The key question is where the contemporary practice of VC financing fits within the PLS techniques of Islamic finance. Two alternative approaches that might be used for Islamic VC are now explored in greater depth.

In an effort to overcome the problems described above, mudarabah has been combined with another financial structure, wakalah, whereby clients authorise a bank or fund manager to invest funds on their behalf, in return for a predetermined fee. This structure is widely used by Islamic mutual funds (Iqbal and Molyneux, 2005) and a combined TTM-Wakalah structure could offer a suitable model for an Islamic VC initiative.

However, there is a major problem to be addressed in mudarabah, deals. In the mudarabah structure, both the financial institution and the recipient can agree on any covenants at the time of the disbursement of the funds. If the project does not proceed as originally planned, then covenants cannot subsequently be changed unless both parties agree. It would be difficult for investor and entrepreneur to resolve disputes on (say) product development, replacing the CEO and so on. The Islamic resistance to changing the terms of the deal stems from the principle that the outcome of the entrepreneur's efforts should not be at the mercy of the capital provider. In rnudarabah structures, therefore, all possible outcomes and their consequences have to be agreed upfront. This arrangement could present problems for the way in which venture capitalists structure the contracts with their investee companies.

The second option for the development of Islamic VC stems from the shiir'ka al-man financial structure (Siddiqi, 1985). In the Ottoman State, the manufacture and trade of fabrics, the production of pillows and shoes were funded in this way (Cizacka, 1996). In shir'ka al-man, two or more members invest a certain amount of capital and share the benefits on a pre-agreed basis. This approach permits the capital provider to place any number of restrictive covenants on the functioning of fund managers and/or entrepreneurs (Fethi, 2000). In the VC context, shir'ka al-inam is a genuine partnership hence both parties are equally involved in any decision to change the strategy of the investee company, even after the disbursement of funds.

The analysis above demonstrates that a hybrid of mudarabah and shir'ka al-man would give capital providers many of the powers available to established venture capitalists; in particular, the investors can insist upon the inclusion of covenants in the contract and they can make post-investment adjustments/interventions to ensure that the investee company stays on course for success. Likewise, mudarabah in conjunction with wakalah provides another option for venture capitalists (albeit less flexible), because the wakeel (representative) may be allowed to carry out business activities within mutually agreed parameters.

The critical question is whether Islamic profit-sharing contracts (musharakah or mudarabah) can provide the required flexibility for efficient risk management. This question can be explored in relation to two fundamental dimensions of the structuring process: contractual structuring (the covenants included in shareholders' agreements and any staging agreements); and, the selection of financial products, namely the choice between equity, debt or hybrids.

In Islamic jurisprudence, parties are free to structure a contract to achieve their mutual economic interests, provided that basic Islamic principles are not violated (Ahmed, 2004). The commonly used covenants in VC shareholders' agreements and/or the conditions tot investment staging could he applied to mudarabah and musharakah structures, provided that such instruments were used in conjunction with shir'ka al-inan or wakalah.

The idea of differential or disproportionate revenue sharing between two classes of 'equity' investors has already been approved in Islamic jurisprudence (Ahmed, 2004). This concession applies provided that the party offering finance also contributes to the management of the project. A modified version of preferred stock could create two classes of shares, with each being entitled to different percentages of profit beyond a defined threshold (Zarqa, 1992). Another financial product that meets the needs of entrepreneurs while simultaneously limiting investment risk is 'diminishing musharakah,' (Bendjijali and Khan, 1985). This structure can be fully secured by using company assets as collateral, thus protecting the original capital to some extent until the project achieves profitability. From cash generated through profits, the entrepreneur can begin to repurchase the equity issued to the venture capitalists. (This arrangement resembles the option in VC deals that gives the entrepreneur the right of first refusal to 'buyback' equity held by outside investors.) Overall, the venture capitalists' return varies according to the investee company's profitability. This gain plus a gradual redemption of part of the invested capital appears Islamically acceptable.

Conventional Venture Capital Practice Shari'ah View (Ahmed H., 2004)

- Limited partnership structure Acceptable.
- Long-terms contracts Acceptable.
- Contracts can be nullified Acceptable.
- Restrictions placed on the activities of fund managers Acceptable.
- Equity ratchets to entrepreneurs Acceptable.
- Investments in equity, fully convertible bonds (zero coupon) Acceptable.
- Preferred stocks, preference shares of convertible debt Not acceptable.

- Greater control rights through restrictive covenants Acceptable.
- Board Seat Acceptable.
- Staged Financing Acceptable.
- Replacement of management (CEO) Acceptable.
- Liquidation rights Acceptable.
- Provision of non-financial services (strategic advice, etc.,) Acceptable.
- Application of discount rate for valuation Acceptable.

Structuring Issues

Even though investing in a venture is an acceptable financial transaction, some aspects of the conventional venture capital structure are not in line with Shari'ah rulings. These aspects are mainly related to preferred stocks and shares that act like a debt instruments. A Shari'ah compliant structure aims to balance the risk/reward benefits to all parties involved in a deal. As such, any financial instrument that acts like a debt security, where the investor can get a 'riskless' reward is prohibited. However, if the burden of risk is placed unevenly on the investor, the investor will not have the incentive to participate in a high risk venture. Two factors aspects are discussed briefly below:

(a) Preferred Stock

In order to minimize the downside risk to Islamic investors, workable preferred stock has been suggested. This 'Islamic' preferred stock acts like a pure preference share with pre-determined varying profit ratios. There can be no accumulation of profits and no liquidity preference to one investor over another in case of sale or liquidation of the venture. Thus it is more like common stock with pre-determined profit rates.

(b) Valuation

Since private equity deals are by nature risky transactions, true valuation of the deal is vital to achieve the target rate of return which is bench-marked against some risk free security, such as US Treasury bonds. Such benchmarks are performance goals against which a company's success is measured, and does not necessarily involve the actual application of riba to a transaction. However, Islamic investors tend to value a company based on two important factors for Shari'ah compliance:

- Returns on a project with a similar risk profile.
- The average return on a well diversified equity portfolio.

Upsurge of Islamic Syndicated Financing

Syndicated lending is a loan provided to a borrower jointly by two or more lenders in the form of a group. The syndicate has become a major feature of conventional financial system. It is an important way of raising large amounts of capital not possible otherwise; lenders are able to diversify their loan portfolios and minimize their risk exposure; these loans are less expensive and are more efficient to administer.

Generally, there are three parties involved in a syndicated loan: the lead manager, the participants, and the borrower. The two main forms of syndicated lending are direct syndication and indirect syndication.

The concept of syndicated loans appeared in the 1960s as a result of efforts to internationalise banking operations. In 2007, the global syndicated loan market was estimated at over $4.5 trillion. Though the current financial crisis has resulted in a decline in syndicated deals, syndicated lending has strong growth potential in both the short and the long-term.

Due to the benefits of syndication for raising capital, it has found its way in Shari' acompliant finance as well. Islamic experts derive the permissibility of syndicated financing from the concept of musharaka. However, due to the prohibition of riba, there are certain differences between Islamic syndicated financing and conventional syndicated lending.

According to the Accounting and Auditing Organization for Islamic Financial Institutions (AAOIFI), Islamic syndicated financing 'refers to the participation of a group of institutions in a joint financing operation through one of the Shari'a-permitted modes of financing.' Just as the modes of finance must be Shari'a-permitted – like ijarah, istisna, mudaraba, murabaha, musharaka, sukuk, etc., – the projects financed through syndication must also be Shari'a compliant.

While it is preferred that syndication should take place among Shari'a-compliant financial institutions, there is no restriction on the participation of conventional financial institutions as long as the arrangement and utilisation of funds and the procedures are in conformity with Islamic principles. The reason is simple: Islam does not prohibit a partnership between a Muslim and a non-Muslim if the activity does not violate the principles given in the Quran and the Sunnah.

Similarly, it is preferred that the syndicate should be led by a Shari'a-compliant financial institution. However, there is nothing against a conventional financial institution acting as the lead manager.

Also, it is not prohibited for Shari'a-compliant financial institutions to provide syndicated financing to certain parts of a venture that is receiving conventional financing for its other parts, provided that the accounts and the lead manager arrangements of the two types of financing are kept strictly separate.

Islamic syndicated financing is one of the sectors of Shari'a-compliant finance that have achieved tremendous growth rates. According to Islamic Finance Information Service (IFIS), the amount of financing showed a 32 per cent increase in 2008: from $19.6 billion in 2007 to $27.2 billion in 2008. However, looking at the financing arrangers and their performances in 2007 and 2008, it becomes obvious that the market does not have established leaders in Islamic syndicated financing. Consequently, there is a lot of room for competition.

Interestingly, Islamic Syndication came to a Halt in the Fourth Quarter of 2008 as Credit Markets all over the world experienced a standstill in that period. Still, the prospects of Islamic syndicated financing are bright. In the GCC countries, the huge infrastructure projects planned over the next ten years are enough to keep the industry going comfortably. And if we add to this, the credit requirements of different corporations in the region along with Islamic syndication taking place outside the Middle East, the scenario looks quite promising.

CHAPTER

Shariah Supervision in Modern Islamic Finance

Shariah supervision may be thought of as the single most important distinction between a conventional and a truly Islamic financial venture. For, while a business may attempt to represent itself as 'Islamic', unless it has qualified Shariah supervision, it has no way of certifying that its services, products, and operations are actually Shariah-compliant. In the emerging Islamic financial sector, therefore, Shariah supervision is not a matter to be taken lightly. Public confidence, in any sector, is always an important consideration; and in the financial sector its importance is paramount. Shari'ah supervision signifies a real commitment on the part of management to the principles of transparency and accountability in the matter of Shari'ah compliance.

What is Shariah Supervision?

While it may be convenient to explain Shari'ah supervision as a religious audit (especially to Western observers and regulators), its scope is far more comprehensive. In essence, Shari'ah supervision is the process of ensuring that a financial product or service complies with Islamic legal precepts and principles, either by its conforming (to one degree or another) to a recognised Islamic legal norm or by its not violating the same. Ideally, Shari'ah supervision will be a part of an Islamic product or service from the time of its development, to its launch, and throughout the period it is offered. At the stage of research and development, or of drafting contracts or offering memorandums, Shari'ah supervision, in one form or another, should be an active participant. By including Shari'ah supervision and advice at the earliest stages, management may save costly legal fees that may be required at a later stage if elements of the proposed business/contracts need to be modified to comply with Shari'ah principles and precepts.

Generally speaking, if Shari'ah supervisors are to certify a venture, they will insist on being a part of its development; or at least to having access to the details of whatever went into the development or structuring of the product, instrument, service, or enterprise. Moreover, once a product is launched, Shari'ah supervision may take the form of ongoing monitoring through periodic audits. Such audits may be undertaken by means of site visits, document reviews, or consultation with management at regular intervals.

Purpose

The most obvious and immediate purpose of Shari'ah supervision is to certify for practicing Muslim consumers and clients that the financial product or service being offered to them is acceptable from an Islamic legal perspective and is therefore lawful to them. Such certification, generally documented in a formal fatwa (Shari'ah position paper), may be thought of as a form of due diligence. In effect, the Shari'ah supervisor, or supervisory board, performs this due diligence on behalf of consumers who are without access to the details of what is offered to them and, likewise, without the experience or qualifications to evaluate those details in light of Shari'ah teachings. By assuming responsibility for the Shari'ah compliance of an Islamic financial institution, including its policies and practices, Shari'ah supervision places itself in a position of directly representing the religious interests of the Muslim investor or consumer; and by making every possible effort to ensure that an Islamic financial product is halal, the services performed by Shari'ah supervisors are directed toward the investor, or the consumer. Undoubtedly, as a result of these efforts, Islamic financial institutions and their management will also benefit. But certainly the primary beneficiary is the Muslim consumer who can rest assured that his/her money is being put to use in ways that accord with the teachings of Islam. It is for this reason that Shari'ah supervision may also be characterised as consumer advocacy.

Background

Since many if not most of the dealings or operations of Islamic banks may be considered novel, in the sense that these were unknown in the times of the classical jurists, there is a very real need for reliable opinions on these dealings; legal and academic opinions derived from authentic Shari'ah sources by the means and methodologies established by generations of Muslim jurists. Then, while it may indeed be possible for an individual to come up with authoritative opinions on these issues, it soon became clear to the newly established Islamic banks that it would be better to have the collective opinions of a group of scholars. Moreover, the banks soon learned that it was best to appoint scholars with specialisations in the field of fiqh al mu'amalat, and who also had working knowledge of modern financial markets and practices. Then, by means of qualified Shari'ah supervision, Islamic banks may assure their clients and investors that the operations they undertake are reviewed in all of their details for compliance with the principles and precepts of the Shari'ah. By means of such a review, by such a group of experts, the banks and financial institutions may clearly demonstrate that their transactions and dealings conform to Islamic legal norms.

Elements of Shari'ah Supervision: Numbers

Shari'ah supervision may be performed by an individual supervisor/advisor, or by a board of supervisors/advisors, commonly known as a Shari'ah Supervisory Board. Whether an institution has a board or a single supervisor is its own choice. Generally speaking, however, such a choice is informed by several considerations. Chief among these considerations is the product or operation itself. An Islamic home financing alternative, for example, is a complex affair and will undoubtedly benefit from the collective opinions of a diversified Shari'ah Board. The same will be true of a commercial or investment banking operation. An Islamic mutual fund, on the other hand, may require a single supervisor, especially if it has licensed itself to an index provider like the Dow Jones Islamic Market Indexes, and is set up to do no more than track the index. An actively managed fund, however, even if it is licensed to an index, may require more than one supervisor. These are considerations that have to do with the nature and requirements of the supervision itself. At the same time, marketing considerations may also be of importance to management. If a product or service is to be marketed internationally, for example, or in a market in which Muslims from different parts of the world are found (like the US and UK), then it may be in the interest of management to engage several scholars, each from a different part of the Muslim world. Whatever the case, prudence dictates that there be at least three supervisors for any Islamic financial undertaking. Moreover, experience has shown that at least one of the members needs to reside in the same country or region as the operation, so as to be readily available for consultation, even on short notice. In some cases, too, a Shari'ah supervisor will maintain an office and keep regular hours at the bank or financial institution.

Elements of Shari'ah Supervision: Qualifications

Obviously, a Shari'ah supervisor will be someone with a background in the classical Shari'ah sciences. In particular, however, supervisors need to have studied the fiqh al mu'amalat or rules concerning transactions developed by the classical jurists and expanded upon by later generations of Shari'ah scholars. Most Shari'ah supervisors have produced academic work or studies on one aspect or another of these rules. In addition, such a background presupposes facility in the classical Arabic language and the ability to deal directly with legal texts, glosses, and commentaries in that language. In addition to all this, an understanding of modern finance, markets, and economics is also clearly required. Finally, an effective Shari'ah supervisor must be familiar with international business practices ('urf) and have an appreciation for regulatory environments. For these reasons, the English language is especially important. One more point that should be kept in mind is the supervisor's ability to work with a team, often times in a cross-disciplinary and cross-cultural environment.

Generally speaking, today's Shari'ah supervisors possess the qualifications and characteristics discussed above. In addition, many Shari'ah supervisors have benefited from the exposure afforded by multiple board membership. Then, while at the present time there are no standard qualifications for Shari'ah supervisors, it is to be hoped that, in the future, and as the Islamic financial sector grows, graduate level programmes will be developed for the specific purpose of preparing new generations of scholars with all of the requisite skills. At present, however, the number of people qualified to serve as Shari'ah supervisors is limited. My own suggestion in regard to preparing scholars for a future in Shari'ah supervision is twofold.

Firstly, Islamic financial operations may appoint, in addition to its full Shari'ah Board members, junior members who will participate in discussions, prepare memos and briefs, take notes, and perform research and other tasks for the Shari'ah Board, but who will not have full status as voting Shari'ah Board members.

Secondly, junior members may be appointed on a rotating basis, such that each will serve, much like a law clerk for a serving judge in the United States, for a period of one year. By means of this rotating arrangement, many scholars will have an opportunity to learn first hand about the workings of Shari'ah supervision. Moreover, as junior members become increasingly more familiar with modern business norms and practices, it will become easier for them to analyze situations and think through options, with the result that their contributions to the work of the Shari'ah Supervisory Boards will become increasingly valuable. Obviously, such junior members will be compensated for their efforts, though not at the same level as the full board members.

Elements of Shari'ah Supervision: Independence

In order to be effective, Shari'ah supervision must be independent. In addition, the decisions of the supervisor/s must be binding on management. If these steps are not taken, the credibility of the supervision, and the company, will be in question. The recommendation of AAOIFI is that Shari'ah supervision must serve at the pleasure of the company's Board of Directors, and not be subject to management. Under such an arrangement, the Board will be free to approve or disapprove of what management does, or proposes to do, solely on the basis of Shari'ah/legal considerations. Of course, this is not to say that a Shari'ah Board will automatically become a thorn in the side of management. On the contrary, most Shari'ah Boards operate in the spirit of co-operation and accommodation.

Elements of Shari'ah Supervision: Communication

An essential element in the success of any undertaking is communication. This is equally true in regard to Shari'ah supervision. To begin with, there must be clearly delineated lines of communication between management and Shari'ah supervision. Often times, an Islamic financial institution will appoint one of its executives, whether from business operations, finance, or legal, to act as liaison with the supervision. This person will be responsible for coordinating and documenting regular meetings, arranging for the requirements of Shari'ah supervision, following up on decisions and suggestions, and processing and channeling communications to and from supervision. When board members live on different continents and work in different time zones, the work of such a co-ordinator can be challenging.

Elements of Shari'ah Supervision: Education

The correlate of consumer advocacy is consumer education. In making this observation I mean to refer to the world of possibilities for enhancing Muslim consumer awareness of, and appreciation for, Islamic financial services and products. For example, the Dow Jones Market Indexes developed and supported a course on the Principles of Islamic Investing that was offered to students of the Dow Jones University on the internet. Unfortunately, the course is no longer available, though efforts are underway for its revival at another venue. Likewise, several Islamic financial institutions supported the effort to produce the *Guide to Islamic Investing* in co-operation with the Lightbulb Press; and others are supporting the *Guide to Islamic Home Acquisition.* In short, every institution offering Islamic financial services needs to concern itself, to one degree or another, with issues of Consumer education. Obviously, the chief concern will be to provide information about their own products. But, generally speaking, Muslim consumers need to know that Islamic financial alternatives exist. They need to know that these alternatives are viable, from both a religious viewpoint and a practical one. And they need to know that these are competitive and worthy of their trust. These are the basics of such an education. Obviously, there is much more that can be done. In a service-oriented market that is driven by competition, the firms with the better services will have the most success. Shari'ah supervision that engages in consumer education enhances service, not to mention consumer confidence.

Shari'ah Supervision Then and Now

As the sector goes, so goes its Shari'ah supervision. Perhaps nothing could be more obvious. In the days when Islamic banking was in its infancy, Shari'ah supervision, too, was feeling its way. With little or no exposure to modern finance, Shari'ah supervisors faced a very steep learning curve. To begin with, in the fifties and sixties, there was very little in terms of literature on the subject. The State Banks of a handful of Muslim countries sponsored conferences on 'Islamic Economics' and Shari'ah scholars were invited to contribute. These early papers and presentations led to more concerted efforts and scholarship. With the advent of Islamic banking in the seventies, and a real demand for Shari'ah supervision, there was more incentive for such academic efforts. Indeed, the development of the sector, and the development of the various sets of expertise required to give it momentum went hand in hand. Today, after the passing of over thirty years since the first Islamic banks opened their doors for business, Shari'ah supervision continues to improve and evolve. Globally, a number of different efforts to increase our understanding of Islamic finance are underway. Universities offer courses on various subjects in Islamic Finance today, not only Economics; and several important graduate dissertations have been published in English and Arabic. Journals on the subject of Islamic finance are published regularly. Websites devoted to the subject are available on the internet. Learned academic bodies like the OIC Fiqh Academy in Jedda, AAOIFI in Bahrain, the IIBI in London, the IIIT in Cairo, and the Fiqh Academy in India have produced volumes of literature on the subject; and everywhere scholars are at work. Recently, at a conference on Islamic Finance in Dubai, a welcome step was taken to promote the efforts of individual scholars. This was the 'New Voices' competition, sponsored by the US-based Guidance Financial Group, in which scholars were invited to submit their original work to a jury of experts; and the best paper was awarded a substantial dollar prize.

My own experience has led me to a view of the future of Shari'ah supervision that includes increasingly informed discourse by enlightened Shari'ah scholarship. It may be difficult to achieve consensus on every issue, but the important thing is that our Shari'ah scholars are now able to speak with authority on these issues. Moreover, cross disciplinary collaboration on projects in which there is active participation by lawyers, Shari'ah scholars, and business professionals will bring more innovation to the industry and further enrich the emerging academic discourse.

Innovation and creative thinking have always been a part of development; and it is clear that the Islamic financial industry is developing in ways, and on a scale, that were unimaginable only a few decades ago.

The Importance of Shariah Supervision in Islamic Financial Institutions

Islamic financial institutions are guided by a legitimate control body known as the *Shari'ah* Supervisory Board (SSB). The purpose of the SSB is to ensure that the financial institutions operate in conformity with *Shari'ah* and are usually made up of a number of jurists who provide clarification in regards to any questions that the financial institutions may have (Usmani 1998). These SSBs consist of *Shari'ah* advisers who are hired by the financial institutions and act as an internal control body in the organization, therefore, enhancing the credibility of the institutions in the eyes of its customers, and bolstering their Islamic credentials.

Although nearly all organizations dealing with Islamic products utilise the services of a religious scholar, the level of involvement of the adviser varies depending on the size of the institution. Thus, large organizations tend to hire a board, whereas smaller organizations dealing with Islamic products would hire the services of just one adviser. A review of four Islamic financial institution's website was undertaken to determine the structure of the SSBs in different organizations around the world. These institutions were:

1. Muslim Community Co-operative Australia (MCCA)-Australia.
2. Iskan Finance-Australia.
3. Meezan Bank-Pakistan
4. LaRiba American Finance House-USA.

This sample revealed that Iskan finance did not have a *Shari'ah* adviser or SSB, instead the organization models its programmes on the various *fatwas* issued by leading Islamic scholars, and on opinions it seeks from Al Azhar University in Egypt (Iskan 2004). MCCA, the largest Islamic financial services provider in Australia (Saeed 2001), has two *Shari'ah* advisers (MCCA 2004), whereas LaRiba relies on one resident *Shari'ah* adviser (LaRiba 2004). Meezan Bank, the first scheduled Islamic commercial bank in Pakistan, relies on a SSB whose members are also on other boards around the world, including the Dow Jones Islamic Index (Meezan 2004).

The presence of a *Shari'ah* board in Islamic banks was determined as a prerequisite for admission into the International Association of Islamic Banks (IAIB). The general characteristics of the *Shari'ah* Board were described in an IAIB document by El-Nagar (1980). According to the document, a *Shari'ah* board should be formed of a number of members chosen from among Jurists and men of Islamic jurisprudence and of comparative law who have conviction and firm belief in the idea of Islamic Banks. To ensure freedom of initiating the board's opinion, members of the board must not be working as personnel in the bank, and are not subject to the authority of the board of directors. The board should be appointed by the general assembly, as it is the case of the auditors of accounts, and the general assembly should fix their remuneration. And finally according to the IAIB document, the board has the same means and jurisdictions as the auditors of accounts.

Banaga, Ray and Tomkins (1994, pp. 10-11) list the functions of the SSB as:

- Answering the enquiries that come from the community at large.
- Issuing formal legal opinions according to the Islamic law and enquiries submitted by bank management or any other interested party.
- Reviewing and revising all the dealings and transactions, which the bank enters into which clients so as to ensure that these agree with *Shari'ah*. If any deals or transactions contradict *Shari'ah* principles, such transactions would not be approved.
- Reviewing researchers on any particular subject and issuing their opinion.

- Holding regular meetings to discuss all enquiries received. The minutes of these meetings are usually recorded.
- Receiving enquiries from the management or others and presenting them to the board of directors.
- Preparing draft opinions and delivering them to all those who are concerned.
- Issuing opinions in final form if the Board does not have any second opinion on the subject.
- Preparing contracts in collaboration with the legal adviser of the bank.
- Participating in the preparation of drafts of decrees, decisions and orders presented by the bank, and preparing explanatory notes there to.
- Preparing the studies and researches required to direct the *zakat* resources towards the deserving parties and determining the rate or the percentage that in the light of the *Shari'ah* rules could be invested from the resources of the *zakat.*
- Carrying out the technical review and follow up to make sure that the *Shari'ah* controls are implemented by the bank, its branches and its affiliated companies.

Zakat is the amount of money that every adult, mentally stable, free, and financially able Muslim, male and female, has to pay to support specific categories people. Zakat is obligatory after a time span of one lunar year passes with the money in the control of it's owner. Then the owner needs to pay 2.5 per cent (or 1/40) of the money as Zakat. (A lunar year is approximately 355 days).

The role of the SSB is therefore similar to that of the account auditors. Even though, the financial institution compensates them, the SSB members are expected to retain their independence. Just like auditors, SSBs certify at the end of the year whether the financial institutions operations were in conformity with *Shari'ah*. This task includes reviewing products and policies of the financial institution, and deciding on whether a new financial instrument introduced by the organization is religiously acceptable.

According to Lewis and Algaoud (2001, p. 181), when the SSB feels that a transaction may not accord fully with, or be in breach of the *Shari'ah,* the board should find alternative ways to make the transaction accord with *Shari'ah.* If no alternative suggestions can be made, the transaction should not be processed. If, however, the transaction has been executed and later on it is discovered that it has violated *Shari'ah,* the SSB should put its qualified opinion to shareholders and the management make steps to take out the income generated from that transaction from the income account and have it distributed to a charity account. There is thus a potential financial penalty for non-compliance as well as adverse publicity.

Theoretically if the SSB refuses to endorse a product, the financial institution should automatically scrap that product. Also in theory, the SSB would perform a religious audit of all accounts (Warde 2000). The reality however is more complicated. A survey conducted by Warde (1998) revealed that in many cases the review is treated as a routine matter, with boards approving decisions already made by the bank's management.

The exact roles of SSBs differ between institutions. Although SSBs have similar supervisory procedures; there remain differences in interpretation. Karim (1990, p. 39) points this out by stating that SSBs 'are guided by their moral beliefs and obligations to religious peers and community'.

Issues Relating to the Working of SSBs

A number of issues have been raised in connection with SSBs. One is in relation to their independence. Since SSB members receive remuneration from the financial institution, there seems to exist a potential for conflict of interest. The concern is that members of the SSB may legitimize dubious operations to ensure that they remain active on the board.

Another issue is that of the relationship between the SSBs and the external auditors.

Some observers believe that since SSBs are present in financial institutions, the external auditors are not qualified to contribute to religious supervision. Others argue that the external auditors are necessary since they act as an external control body that ensures that the financial institutions are adhering to *Shari'ah* (Usmani 2001). In studies conducted by Algaoud and Lewis (1997, 1999) it was revealed that the Islamic banks had no formal interaction between the SSBs and the external auditors.

There have also been questions asked about the need for SSBs. With employees of financial institutions now being able to access the latest research and training programmes related to Islamic finance from organizations such as the Institute of Islamic Banking and Insurance, the presence of SSBs is viewed by some as fulfillment of a formality rather than an active control body (Warde 2000).

In relation to the global growth and application of Islamic finance, the major criticism is that the practice of financial institutions having their own *Shari'ah* boards adds to the differences in application. This makes it difficult to agree on globally acceptable products and procedures. For example, some financial institutions have been guaranteeing profits and effectively taking the risk factor out of the financial transactions. Thus the guaranteed return resembles interest rather than a *halal* payment.

Role of Central Banks and Regulatory Bodies

Differences in application and procedures not only exist between nations but also within a nation. To overcome the concerns about SSBs, the Islamic finance community can undertake a number of steps to standardise activities at the national and international levels. According to Warde (2000), this can be achieved by placing more emphasis on encouraging group *Ijtihad* through international conferences, symposia, and convocations. By bringing people together from around the world, there can be more opportunities for discussions on the grey areas in Islamic finance, and for possible consensus on the global practice and applications of the system (Siddiqi 1994).

At the national level, the Central banks of the Muslim countries have to take a more proactive role in order to co-ordinate activities within the national boundaries (Gafoor 1996). There are already moves being made in this direction with some central banks appointing their own *Shari'ah* advisers to oversee national operations. One of the most significant attempts at national harmonization occurred in Malaysia where a National Syariah (*Shari'ah*) Board was established in 1997 to harmonize financial practices and review the compatibility of new financial products with religion, as well as advise the Central Bank on religious matters. A similar move has recently been made by the State Bank of Pakistan, which has established an Islamic Banking Unit. But despite of these efforts, the two nations differ in their application of Islamic finance. While Malaysia is pursuing a dual finance system where both conventional and Islamic financing options will be available, the Pakistani government has in the past tried to enforce Islamic finance as the only available option.

Finally, to streamline activities at the international level, regulatory bodies need to be formed and policies made that would ensure uniformity in procedure and applications. The recently formed Islamic Financial Services Board (IFSB) aims to do just that. The IFSB serves as an international standard setting body of the regulatory and supervisory agencies that have vested interest in ensuring the soundness and stability of the Islamic financial services industry.

The establishment of the IFSB in Malaysia in late 2002 was the result of a two-year consultative process initiated by a group of governors and senior officials of central banks of various countries, together with the support from the Islamic Development Bank, the International Monetary Fund, and the Accounting and Auditing Organization for Islamic Financial Institutions. The IFSB is at currently attempting to prepare a standard on Corporate Governance, and has also begun on development of two prudential standards for the Islamic financial services industry namely, Capital Adequacy and Risk Management standards (IFSB 2004).

The IFSB is in its infancy stage, and its effectiveness will become clearer over time.

By regulating the system, including the activities of the SSBs, through an active participation of academics, scholars, Central banks, and regulatory bodies, there is hope that Islamic financial system can be streamlined and criticism leveled against the system can be deflected.

CHAPTER

10

Micro-finance

Micro-finance refers to the provision of financial services to low-income clients, including consumers and the self-employed. More broadly, it refers to a movement that envisions "a world in which as many poor and near-poor households as possible have permanent access to an appropriate range of high quality financial services, including not just credit but also savings, insurance, and fund transfers". Those who promote micro-finance generally believe that such access will help poor people out of poverty.

The Challenge

Traditionally, banks have not provided financial services to clients with little or no cash income. Banks must incur substantial costs to manage a client account, regardless of how small the sums of money involved. For example, the total revenue from delivering one hundred loans worth $1,000 each will not differ greatly from the revenue that results from delivering one loan of $100,000. But the fixed cost of processing loans – of any size – is considerable: assessment of potential borrowers, their repayment prospects and security; administration of outstanding loans, collecting from delinquent borrowers and so on. There is a break-even point in providing loans or deposits below which banks lose money on each transaction they make. Poor people usually fall below it.

In addition, most poor people have few assets that can be secured by a bank as collateral. As documented extensively by Hernando de Soto and others, even if they happen to own land in the developing world, they may not have effective title to it. This means that the bank will have little recourse against defaulting borrowers.

Seen from a broader perspective, it has long been accepted that the development of a healthy national financial system is an important goal and catalyst for the broader goal of national economic development (see for example Alexander Gerschenkron, Paul Rosenstein-Rodan, Joseph Schumpeter, Anne Krueger etc.). However, the efforts of national planners and experts to develop financial services for their nations' majorities have often failed since World War II, for reasons summarised well by Adams, Graham and Von Pischke in their classic analysis 'Undermining Rural Development with Cheap Credit'.

Because of these difficulties, when poor people borrow they often rely on relatives or a local moneylender, whose interest rates can be very high. An analysis of 28 studies of informal moneylending rates in fourteen countries in Asia, Latin America and Africa concluded that 76 per cent of moneylender rates exceed 10 per cent per month, including 22 per cent that exceed 100 per cent per month. Moneylenders usually charge higher rates to poorer borrowers than to less poor ones. While moneylenders are often demonised and accused of usury, their services are convenient and fast, and they can be very flexible when borrowers run into problems. Hopes of quickly putting them out of business have proven unrealistic, even in places where micro-finance institutions are very active.

Over the past centuries practical visionaries from the Franciscan monks who founded the community-oriented pawnshops of the fifteenth century, to the founders of the European credit union movement in the nineteenth century (such as Friedrich Wilhelm Raiffeisen) and the founders of the micro-credit movement in the 1970s (such as Muhammad Yunus) have tested practices and built institutions designed to bring the kinds of livelihood opportunities and risk management tools that financial services provide to the doorsteps of poor people. While the success of Grameen Bank (which now serves over seven million poor Bangladeshi women) has inspired the world, it has proved difficult to replicate this success in practice. In nations with lower population densities, meeting the operating costs of a retail branch by serving nearby customers has proven considerably more challenging.

Although much progress has been made, the problem has not been solved yet, and the overwhelming majority of people who earn less than $1 a day, especially in the rural areas, continue to have no practical access to formal sector finance. Micro-finance has been growing rapidly with $25B currently at work in micro-finance loans. It is estimated that the industry needs $250 billion to get capital to all the poor people who need it. The industry has been growing rapidly and there have been concerns that the rate of capital flowing into micro-finance is a potential risk unless managed well.

Boundaries and Principles

Theoretically, micro-finance may encompass any efforts to increase access to, or improve the quality of, financial services poor people currently use or could benefit from using. For example, poor people borrow from informal moneylenders and save with informal collectors. They receive loans and grants from charities. They buy insurance from state-owned companies. They receive funds transfers through remittance networks (like Hawala).

There are not many bright lines that can sharply distinguish micro-finance from similar activities. Claims could be made that a government that orders state banks to open deposit accounts for poor consumers, or a moneylender that engages in usury, or a charity that runs a heifer pool are engaged in micro-finance. Furthermore, correcting the problem of access is best done by expanding the number of financial institutions available to them, as well as the capacity of those institutions. In recent years there has been increasing emphasis on expanding the diversity of those institutions as well, since different institutions serve different needs.

Some principles that summarise a century and a half of development practice were encapsulated in 2004 by Consultative Group to Assist the Poor (CGAP) and endorsed by the Group of Eight leaders at the G8 Summit on June 10, 2004:

- Poor people need not just loans but also savings, insurance and money transfer services.
- Micro-finance must be useful to poor households: helping them raise income, build up assets and/or cushion themselves against external shocks.
- 'Micro-finance can pay for itself'. Subsidies from donors and government are scarce and uncertain, and so to reach large numbers of poor people, micro-finance must pay for itself.
- Micro-finance means building permanent local institutions.
- Micro-finance also means integrating the financial needs of poor people into a country's mainstream financial system.
- "The job of government is to enable financial services, not to provide them".
- "Donor funds should complement private capital, not compete with it".
- "The key bottleneck is the shortage of strong institutions and managers". Donors should focus on capacity building.
- Interest rate ceilings hurt poor people by preventing micro-finance institutions from covering their costs, which chokes off the supply of credit.
- Micro-finance institutions should measure and disclose their performance – both financially and socially.

Micro-finance can also be distinguished from charity. It is better to provide grants to families who are destitute, or so poor they are unlikely to be able to generate the cash flow required to repay a loan. This situation can occur for example, in a war zone or after a natural disaster.

Debates at the Boundaries

There are several key debates at the boundaries of micro-finance.

Practitioners and donors from the charitable side of micro-finance frequently argue for restricting micro-credit to loans for productive purposes – such as to start or expand a micro-enterprise. Those from the private-sector side respond that because money is fungible, such a restriction is impossible to enforce, and that in any case it should not be up to rich people to determine how poor people use their money.

Perhaps influenced by traditional Western views about usury, the role of the traditional moneylender has been subject to much criticism, especially in the early stages of modern micro-finance. As more poor people gained access to loans from micro-credit institutions however, it became apparent that the services of moneylenders continued to be valued. Borrowers were prepared to pay very high interest rates for services like quick loan disbursement, confidentiality and flexible repayment schedules. They did not always see lower interest rates as adequate compensation for the costs of attending meetings, attending training courses to qualify for disbursements or making monthly collateral contributions. They also found it distasteful to be forced to pretend they were borrowing to start a business, when they were often borrowing for other reasons (such as paying for school fees, dealing with health costs or securing the family food supply). The more recent focus on inclusive financial systems (see section below) affords moneylenders more legitimacy, arguing in favour of regulation and efforts to increase competition between them to expand the options available to poor people.

Modern micro-finance emerged in the 1970s with a strong orientation towards private-sector solutions. This resulted from evidence that state-owned agricultural development banks in developing countries had been a monumental failure, actually undermining the development goals they were intended to serve (see the compilation edited by Adams, Graham and Von Pischke). Nevertheless public officials in many countries hold a different view, and continue to intervene in micro-finance markets.

There has been a long-standing debate over the sharpness of the trade-off between 'outreach' (the ability of a micro-finance institution to reach poorer and more remote people) and its 'sustainability' (its ability to cover its operating costs – and possibly also its costs of serving new clients – from its operating revenues). Although it is generally agreed that micro-finance practitioners should seek to balance these goals to some extent, there are a wide variety of strategies, ranging from the minimalist profit-orientation of BancoSol in Bolivia to the highly integrated not-for-profit orientation of BRAC in Bangladesh. This is true not only for individual institutions, but also for governments engaged in developing national micro-finance systems.

Micro-finance experts generally agree that women should be the primary focus of service delivery. Evidence shows that they are less likely to default on their loans than men. Industry data from 2006 for 704 MFIs reaching 52 million borrowers includes MFIs using the solidarity lending methodology (99.3% female clients) and MFIs using individual lending (51% female clients). The delinquency rate for solidarity lending was 0.9 per cent after 30 days (individual lending – 3.1%), while 0.3 per cent of loans were written off (individual lending – 0.9%). Because operating margins become tighter the smaller the loans delivered, many MFIs consider the risk of lending to men to be too high. This focus on women is questioned sometimes, however. A recent study of micro-enterpreneurs from Sri Lanka published by the World Bank found that the return on capital for male-owned businesses (half of the sample) averaged 11 per cent, whereas the return for women-owned businesses was 0 per cent or slightly negative.

Micro-financial services are needed everywhere, including the developed world. However, in developed economies intense competition within the financial sector, combined with a diverse mix of different types of financial institutions with different missions, ensures that most people have access to some financial services. Efforts to transfer micro-finance innovations such as solidarity lending from developing countries to developed ones have met with little success.

Financial Needs of Poor People

In developing economies and particularly in the rural areas, many activities that would be classified in the developed world as financial are not monetised: that is, money is not used to carry them out. Almost by definition, poor people have very little money. But circumstances often arise in their lives in which they need money or the things money can buy.

In Stuart Rutherford's recent book *The Poor and Their Money*, he cites several types of needs:

- *Lifecycle Needs*: Such as weddings, funerals, childbirth, education, homebuilding, widowhood, old age.
- *Personal Emergencies*: Such as sickness, injury, unemployment, theft, harassment or death.
- *Disasters*: Such as fires, floods, cyclones and man-made events like war or bulldozing of dwellings.
- *Investment Opportunities*: Expanding a business, buying land or equipment, improving housing, securing a job (which often requires paying a large bribe), etc.

Poor people find creative and often collaborative ways to meet these needs, primarily through creating and exchanging different forms of non-cash value. Common substitutes for cash vary from country to country but typically include livestock, grains, jewellery and precious metals.

As Marguerite Robinson describes in The Micro-finance Revolution, the 1980s demonstrated that 'micro-finance could provide large-scale outreach profitably', and in the 1990s, 'micro-finance began to develop as an industry' (2001, p. 54). In the 2000s, the micro-finance industry's objective is to satisfy the unmet demand on a much larger scale, and to play a role in reducing poverty. While much progress has been made in developing a viable, commercial micro-finance sector in the last few decades, several issues remain that need to be addressed before the industry will be able to satisfy massive worldwide demand. The obstacles or challenges to building a sound commercial micro-finance industry include:

- Inappropriate donor subsidies.
- Poor regulation and supervision of deposit-taking MFIs.
- Few MFIs that meet the needs for savings, remittances or insurance.
- Limited management capacity in MFIs.
- Institutional inefficiencies.
- Need for more dissemination and adoption of rural, agricultural micro-finance methodologies.

Ways in which poor People Manage their Money

Rutherford argues that the basic problem poor people as money managers face is to gather a 'usefully large' amount of money. Building a new home may involve saving and protecting diverse building materials for years until enough are available to proceed with construction. Children's schooling may be funded by buying chickens and raising them for sale as needed for expenses, uniforms, bribes, etc. Because all the value is accumulated before it is needed, this money management strategy is referred to as 'saving up'.

Often people don't have enough money when they face a need, so they borrow. A poor family might borrow from relatives to buy land, from a moneylender to buy rice, or from a micro-finance institution to buy a sewing machine. Since these loans must be repaid by saving after the cost is incurred, Rutherford calls this 'saving down'. Rutherford's point is that micro-credit is addressing only half the problem, and arguably the less important half: poor people borrow to help them save and accumulate assets. Micro-credit institutions should fund their loans through savings accounts that help poor people manage their myriad risks.

Most needs are met through mix of saving and credit. A benchmark impact assessment of Grameen Bank and two other large micro-finance institutions in Bangladesh found that for every $1 they were lending to clients to finance rural non-farm micro-enterprise, about $2.50 came from other sources, mostly their clients' savings. This parallels the experience in the West, in which family businesses are funded mostly from savings, especially during start-up.

Recent studies have also shown that informal methods of saving are very unsafe. For example a study by Wright and Mutesasira in Uganda concluded that "those with no option but to save in the informal sector are almost bound to lose some money – probably around one quarter of what they save there".

The work of Rutherford, Wright and others has caused practitioners to reconsider a key aspect of the micro-credit paradigm: that poor people get out of poverty by borrowing, building micro-enterprises and increasing their income. The new paradigm places more attention on the efforts of poor people to reduce their many vulnerabilities by keeping more of what they earn and building up their assets. While they need loans, they may find it as useful to borrow for consumption as for micro-enterprise. A safe, flexible place to save money and withdraw it when needed is also essential for managing household and family risk.

Current Scale of Micro-finance Operations

No systematic effort to map the distribution of micro-finance has yet been undertaken. A useful recent benchmark was established by an analysis of 'alternative financial institutions' in the developing world in 2004. The authors counted approximately 665 million client accounts at over 3,000 institutions that are serving people who are poorer than those served by the commercial banks. Of these accounts, 120 million were with institutions normally understood to practice micro-finance. Reflecting the diverse historical roots of the movement, however, they also included postal savings banks (318 million accounts), state agricultural and development banks (172 million accounts), financial co-operatives and credit unions (35 million accounts) and specialised rural banks (19 million accounts).

Regionally the highest concentration of these accounts was in India (188 million accounts representing 18 per cent of the total national population). The lowest concentrations were in Latin American and the Caribbean (14 million accounts representing 3 per cent of the total population) and Africa (27 million accounts representing 4 per cent of the total population). Considering that most bank clients in the developed world need several active accounts to keep their affairs in order, these figures indicate that the task the micro-finance movement has set for itself is still very far from finished.

By type of service "savings accounts in alternative finance institutions outnumber loans by about four to one. This is a worldwide pattern that does not vary much by region".

An important source of detailed data on selected micro-finance institutions is the *Micro Banking Bulletin.* At the end of 2006 it was tracking 704 MFIs that were serving 52 million borrowers ($23.3 billion in outstanding loans) and 56 million savers ($15.4 billion in deposits). Of these clients, 70 per cent were in Asia, 20 per cent in Latin America and the balance in the rest of the world.

As yet there are no studies that indicate the scale or distribution of 'informal' micro-finance organizations like ROSCAs and informal associations that help people manage costs like weddings, funerals and sickness. Numerous case studies have been published however, indicating that these organizations, which are generally designed and managed by poor people themselves with little outside help, operate in most countries in the developing world.

'Inclusive Financial Systems'

The micro-credit era that began in the 1970s has lost its momentum, to be replaced by a 'financial systems' approach. While micro-credit achieved a great deal, especially in urban and near-urban areas and with entrepreneurial families, its progress in delivering financial services in less densely populated rural areas has been slow.

The new financial systems approach pragmatically acknowledges the richness of centuries of micro-finance history and the immense diversity of institutions serving poor people in developing world today. It is also rooted in an increasing awareness of diversity of the financial service needs of the world's poorest people, and the diverse settings in which they live and work.

Brigit Helms in her book 'Access for All: Building Inclusive Financial Systems', distinguishes between four general categories of micro-finance providers, and argues for a pro-active strategy of engagement with all of them to help them achieve the goals of the micro-finance movement.

Informal Financial Service Providers

These include moneylenders, pawnbrokers, savings collectors, money-guards, ROSCAs, ASCAs and input supply shops. Because they know each other well and live in the same community, they understand each other's financial circumstances and can offer very flexible, convenient and fast services. These services can also be costly and the choice of financial products limited and very short-term. Informal services that involve savings are also risky; many people lose their money.

Member-owned Organizations

These include self-help groups, credit unions, and a variety of hybrid organizations like 'financial service associations' and CVECAs. Like their informal cousins, they are generally small and local, which means they have access to good knowledge about each others' financial circumstances and can offer convenience and flexibility. Since they are managed by poor people, their costs of operation are low. However, these providers may have little financial skill and can run into trouble when the economy turns down or their operations become too complex. Unless they are effectively regulated and supervised, they can be 'captured' by one or two influential leaders, and the members can lose their money.

NGOs

The Micro-credit Summit Campaign counted 3,316 of these MFIs and NGOs lending to about 133 million clients by the end of 2006. Led by Grameen Bank and BRAC in Bangladesh, Prodem in Bolivia, and FINCA International, headquartered in Washington, DC, these NGOs have spread around the developing world in the past three decades; others, like the Gamelan Council, address larger regions. They have proven very innovative, pioneering banking techniques like solidarity lending, village banking and mobile banking that have overcome barriers to serving poor populations. However, with boards that don't necessarily represent either their capital or their customers, their governance structures can be fragile, and they can become overly dependent on external donors.

Formal Financial Institutions

In addition to commercial banks, these include state banks, agricultural development banks, savings banks, rural banks and non-bank financial institutions. They are regulated and supervised, offer a wider range of financial services, and control a branch network that can extend across the country and internationally. However, they have proved reluctant to adopt social missions, and due to their high costs of operation, often can't deliver services to poor or remote populations. The increasing use of alternative data in credit scoring, such as trade credit is increasing commercial banks' interest in micro-finance.

With appropriate regulation and supervision, each of these institutional types can bring leverage to solving the micro-finance problem. For example, efforts are being made to link self-help groups to commercial banks, to network member-owned organizations together to achieve economies of scale and scope, and to support efforts by commercial banks to 'down-scale' by integrating mobile banking and e-payment technologies into their extensive branch networks.

Micro-credit and the Web

Due to slow progress in developing quality savings services for poor people, peer-to-peer platforms have developed to expand microlending through individual lenders in the developed world. Kiva launched in 2005 (United States), MicroPlace in 2006 (United States), MyC4 in 2007 (Denmark), followed by United Prosperity (United States), 51Give, Wokai (China), Rang De (India) and United Youth Development Organization (United Kingdom) in 2008. The volume channeled through Kiva's peer-to-peer platform is ~87 M USD as of August 2009 (Kiva facilitates approximately $5M in loans each month). In comparison, the needs for micro-credit are estimated about 250 bn USD as of end 2006.

Most experts agree that these funds must be sourced locally in countries that are originating micro-credit, to reduce transaction costs and exchange rate risks.

There have been problems with disclosure on peer-to-peer sites, with some reporting interest rates of borrowers using the flat rate methodology instead of the familiar banking Annual Percentage Rate.. The use of flat rates, which has been outlawed among regulated financial institutions in developed countries, can confuse individual lenders into believing their borrower is paying a lower interest rate than, in fact, they are. A recent industry-wide initiative to bring disclosure to international truth in lending standards has been endorsed by many the key stakeholders in micro-credit pricing. For more information on peer to peer platforms, see micro-credit and the web.

Evidence for Reducing Poverty

Some proponents of micro-finance have asserted, without offering credible evidence, that micro-finance has the power to single-handedly defeat poverty. This assertion has been the source of considerable criticism. In addition, research on the actual effectiveness of micro-finance as a tool for economic development remains slim, in part owing to the difficulty in monitoring and measuring this impact. At the 2008 Innovations for Poverty Action/Financial Access Initiative

Micro-finance Research conference, economist Jonathan Morduch of New York University noted there are only one or two methodologically sound studies of micro-finance's impact.

Sociologist Jon Westover found that much of the evidence on the effectiveness of micro-finance for alleviating poverty is based in anecdotal reports or case studies. He initially found over 100 articles on the subject, but included only the 6 which used enough quantitative data to be representative. One of these studies found that micro-finance reduced poverty. Two others were unable to conclude that micro-finance reduced poverty, although they attributed some positive effects to the programme. Other studies concluded similarly, with surveys finding that a majority of participants feel better about finances with some feeling worse.

In May 2009 the Innovations for Poverty Action in New Haven published a paper which found that those randomized to receive financial training had higher profits, although other effects such as reducing 'the proportion who reported having problems in their business' did not occur.

Micro-finance and Social Interventions

There are currently a few social interventions that have been combined with micro-financing to increase awareness of HIV/AIDS. Such interventions like the "Intervention with Micro-finance for AIDS and Gender Equity" (IMAGE) which incorporates micro-financing with 'The Sisters-for-Life' programme a participatory programme that educates on different gender roles, gender-based violence, and HIV/AIDS infections to strengthen the communication skills and leadership of women. 'The Sisters-for-Life' programme has two phases where phase one consists of ten one-hour training programmes with a facilitator with phase two consisting of identifying a leader amongst the group, train them further, and allow them to implement an Action Plan to their respective centres. Micro-finance has also been combined with business education, and with other packages of health interventions. The Village Organizations of BRAC (NGO) also combine micro-finance with other social interventions.

Other Criticisms

There has also been much criticism of the high interest rates charged to borrowers. The real average portfolio yield cited by the a sample of 704 micro-finance institutions that voluntarily submitted reports to the Micro Banking Bulletin in 2006 was 22.3 per cent annually. However, annual rates charged to clients are higher, as they also include local inflation and the bad debt expenses of the micro-finance institution. Muhammad Yunus has recently made much of this point, and in his latest book argues that micro-finance institutions that charge more than 15 per cent above their long-term operating costs should face penalties.

The role of donors has also been questioned. The Consultative Group to Assist the Poor (CGAP) recently commented that "a large proportion of the money they spend is not effective, either because it gets hung up in unsuccessful and often complicated funding mechanisms (for example, a government apex facility), or it goes to partners that are not held accountable for performance. In some cases, poorly conceived programmes have retarded the development of inclusive financial systems by distorting markets and displacing domestic commercial initiatives with cheap or free money".

There has also been criticism of microlenders for not taking more responsibility for the working conditions of poor households, particularly when borrowers become quasi-wage labourers, selling crafts or agricultural produce through an organization controlled by the MFI. The desire of MFIs to help their borrower diversify and increase their incomes has sparked this type of relationship in several countries, most notably Bangladesh, where hundreds of thousands of borrowers effectively work as wage labourers for the marketing subsidiaries of Grameen Bank or BRAC. Critics maintain that there are few if any rules or standards in these cases governing working hours, holidays, working conditions, safety or child labour, and few inspection regimes to correct abuses. Some of these concerns have been taken up by unions and socially responsible investment advocates.

Bibliography

1. Abdullatif, S. *Awareness of AAOIFI Accounting Standards in the Kingdom of Saudi Arabia*. Paper Presented at the IIUM International Conference on Islamic Banking and Finance: Research and Development: The Bridge between Ideals and Realities Organized IIUM Institute of Islamic Banking and Finance, IIUM, Kuala Lumpur, Malaysia, 23-25 April 2007.
2. Aggrawal, R.K. and Yousef T *"Islamic Banks and Investment Financing"*. Journal of Money, Credit and Banksing 32-1 (2000).
3. Ahmad, A.Y. "*Islamic Banking Modes of Finance*: Proposals for Further Evaluation", in M. Iqbal and R. Wilson (eds.), Islamic Perspectives on Wealth Creation. Edinburgh: Edinburgh University Press, 2005.
4. Ahmad, K. "*Economic Development in an Islamic Framework*", in Khurshid A and Zafar I A (eds.), Islamic Perspectives: Studies in Honour of Mawlana Sayyid Abul A'la Mawdudi. Leicester and Jeddah: Islamic Foundation and Saudi Publishing House, 1980.
5. Ahmad, K. *Islamic Approach to Development: Some Policy Implications.* Islamabad: Institute of Policy Studies, 1994.

6. Asutay, M. "*A Political Economy Approach to Islamic Economics: Bank for International Settlements (BIS)*" (Sept. 2008), BIS Quarterly Review: Bank for International Settlements (BIS) (2008), Annual Report. (Basel, Switzerland: BIS).
7. Calomiris, C. (1998), "*The IMF's Imprudent Role as Lender of Last Resort*", Cato Journal, 17(3), Capital Markets (Washington, DC: IMF).
8. Choudhury, M.A. "*Islamic Venture Capital: A Critical Examination*", Journal of Economic Studies (2001): 28-1.
9. Choudhury, M.A. "*The Humanomic Structure of Islamic Economic Theory: A Critical Review of Literature in Normative and Positive Economics.*" Journal of King Abdulaziz University-Islamic Economics 2 (1990).
10. Claessens, S, and Enricho P (2007), "*Finance and Inequality: Channels and Evidence*", Community Reinvestment Coalition Annual Meeting, Washington, DC. 14 March.
11. *Federal Reserve*, Federal Reserve Bulletin, Jan 2008. Retrieved from www.federal reserve.gov/pubs/
12. Feroz, E.H (2007), *"The Halal way to Social Change"* Islamic Horizons, Forum on Islamic Finance Held on 19-20 April 2008 in the Harvard Law School.
13. Galbraith, J.K. (1972), *The New Industrial State* New York: New American Library.
14. Gamal, M.A. *Islamic Finance: Law, Economics and Practice.* New York: Cambridge University Press, 2006.
15. Ghazali, A.H. *Man is the Basis of the Islamic Strategy for Economic Development.* Jeddah: IRT-Islamic Development Bank, 1994.
16. Guene and E. Mayo (Eds.), *Banking and Social Cohesion: Alternative Responses to a Global Market.* Charlbury, Oxfordshire: Jon Carpenter, 2001.
17. Hamoudi, H.A. "*Muhammad's Social Justice or Muslim Cant? Langdellianism and the Failures of Islamic Finance"*. Cornell International Law Journal 40 (2007).

18. Haneef, M. A. *"Can there be an Economics Based on Religion? The Case of Islamic Economics"*. Post-Autistic Economics Review 34 (Internet Edition) (2005).
19. Hasan, Z. "*Fifty Years of Malaysian Economic Development: Policies and Achievements*". Review of Islamic Economics 11-2 (2007).
20. Hasan, Z. *"Islamic Banking at the Crossroads: Theory vs. Practice*", in M. Iqbal and R. Wilson (Eds.), Islamic Perspectives on Wealth Creation. Edinburgh: Edinburgh University Press, 2005.
21. Herszenhorn, D, and Vikas B (2008), "*A Bipartisan Bid on Mortgage Aid is Gaining Homo-economics"* : School of Government and International Affairs, Durham University, UK.
22. Hoboken. Paper for IFSD Forum, 2007, on *Islamic Microfinance Development: Challenges and Perils of Financial Innovation*" NJ: John Wiley.
23. htt://www.ssrn.com
24. http://papers.ssrn.com/sol3/papers.cfm?abstract_id =1093137#
25. http://www.oecd.org/document/61/0,3343,en_2649_ 201185_
26. http://www.ustreas.gov/ press/releases/
27. International Monetary Fund (2007), *Yearbook*, Washington, DC: IMF.
28. International Monetary Fund (August 2008), *International Financial Statistics* Washington, DC: IMF.
29. International Monetary Fund (May 1998), *World Economic Outlook*, Washington, DC: IMF.
30. Iqbal, M. and M. Philip. *Thirty Years of Islamic Banking: History, Performance and Prospects.* London: Palgrave-Macmillan, 2005.
31. Kahf, M. "*Islamic Economics: Notes on Definition and Methodology*". Review of Islamic Economics 13 (2003). Kansas City, Jackson Hole, Wyoming, August 28-30, pp. 55-96.

32. Khan, I. *Islamic Finance: Relevance and Growth in the Modern Financial Age.* Presentation made at the Islamic Finance Seminar Organized by Harvard Islamic Finance Project at the London School of Economics, London, UK, on 1 February 2007.
33. Kuran, T. "*Behavioural Norms in the Islamic Doctrine of Economics: A Critique*". Journal of Economic Behaviour and Organization (1983).
34. Kuran, T. "*Further Reflections the Behavioural Norms of Islamic Economics*". Journal of Economic Behaviour and Organization (1995).
35. Kuran, T. "*The Genesis of Islamic Economics: A Chapter in the Politics of Muslim Identity*". Social Research 64-2 (1997).
36. Leadbearer, C., "*Rags to Riches: Facts or Fiction*" Financial Times, 30 December, 1986.
37. Mahathir M.M. (1997), "*Highwaymen of the Global Economy*", Wall Street Journal, 3.
38. Maurer, B. "*Engineering an Islamic Future: Speculation on Islamic Financial Alternatives*". Anthropology Today 17-1 (2001 February).
39. Maurer, B. "*Re-formatting the Economy: Islamic-Banking and Finance in World Politics*", in Nelly Lahoud and Anthony H. Johns (Eds.), Islam in World Politics. New York: Rutledge, 2005.
40. Mayer, A.E. "*Islamic Banking and Credit Policies in the Sadat Era: The Social Origin of Islamic Banking in Egypt*". Arab Law Quarterly 1-1 (1985 November).
41. Meltzer, A. (1998), "*Asian Problems and the IMF*", Cato Journal, 17(3), 267-274.
42. Menestrel, M. "*Economic Rationality and Ethical Behaviour: Ethical Business between Venality and Sacrifice.*" Business Ethics: A European Review 11-2 (2002).
43. Mian, A, and Amir S (2008), "*The Consequences of Mortgage Credit Expansion: Micro-Credit in Bangladesh*", Dhaka: Bangladesh Unnayan Parishad.

44. Miskhin, F (1997), "*The Causes and Propagation of Financial Instability: Lessons for Modes: The Experience of Sudanese Islamic Banks*". Review of Islamic Economics 9-2 (2005).
45. Papadimitriou (Ed.), *Stability in the Financial System.* London: Macmillan, 1996.
46. Plender, J. (1998), "*Western Crony Capitalism*", Financial Times, 3-4 October.
47. Sharma, S (2002), "*Is Micro-credit A Macro Trap*"? The Hindu, 25 September.
48. The Economist (1998), "*The Risk Business*", 17 October, p. 21.
49. Wikipedia (2008), "*Grameen Bank*", 2 March.
50. Wikipedia (2008), "*United States Public Debt*", 25 February.
51. www.federalreserve.gov/newsevents/speech/bernanke/20070831a.htm.
52. www.hinduonnet.com/businessline/2002/09/25/stories/2002092500810900.htm.
53. www.nytimes.com/2008/04/02/washington/
54. Yeager, I. B. (1998), "*How to Avoid International Financial Crises*", Cato Journal, 17(3), pp. 257.

Index

A

AAOIFI, 98

AAOIFI Shariah Standard, 119

Access for all, 170

Accounts receivables, 40

Adams, 161

Al Ehsa Special Reality Mudaraba, 101

Al Muthanna Investment Company, 103

Annual Percentage Rate, 172

ARDC, 122

Ariyah, 70

ASCAs, 170

B

Bahrain Financial Harbour, 115

Bank for International Settlement (BIS), 16

BIB, 109

BRAC in Bangladesh, 165, 173

Business Cycle Dating Committee, 6

C

Capital Funds, 133

CDO, 13, 16, 138

CFI, 43

CGAP, 163, 174

Chemical Bank, 125

Clinton Administration the Community Redevelopment Act, 12

Coca-Cola Company, 123

Contract is Islamic law, 53

Credit Default Swaps (CDSs), 17

Crisis of success, 5

CVECAs, 170

D

DJIM, 81

Dow Jones Industrial Average Index, 15

Dow Jones Market Indexes, 151

E

Eastern Air Lines, 121

Ed Balls, 94

Edwards, 50

EIRs, 128

ERISA, 124

Euro Zone, 22

European Central Bank, 49

F

FDI, 20

Fed Funds, 12

Federal Home Loan Mortgage Corporation, 12
Federal National Mortgage Association, 12
Federal Republic of Germany, 113
Federal Reserve, 12
Financial crisis of 2007-10, 10-14
FINCA, 171
FTSE Global Islamic Index Series, 84
FTSE Global Islamic Index, 40

G

GCC, 43, 143
GDP, 6, 7
Gharar, 91
Global economic recession, 2
Global financial recession, 4-22
    after effect of crisis in United States and other advanced economies, 17-22
    financial crisis of 2007-10, 10-14
    great depression (1930), 9, 15
    history and evolution, 8
    important global economic crisis-at a glance session 1920's, 15
    October 19th 1987-black Monday, 15-16
    oil crisis, stagflation and Vietnam (1970), 15
    recession and its attributes, 7-8
    recession (1980), 15
        definition, 6-7
        in 2000s, 9-10
    root of the current global financial crisis, 16-17
    some characteristics of a recession, 14-15
    stock market crash (1929), 15
    what is recession, 4-6
Government of Bahrain, 109
Government of Qatar, 98
Grameen Bank, 167, 174
Great Depression, 9
Great Recession, 9, 10, 15
Group of Eight Leaders, 163
GSEs, 12
Guidance Financial Group, 152

H

Hanafis, 58
HIV/AIDS, 173
Hiwalah (transfer of debt), 71
HMC, 98
How Islamic finance as a solution for global financial crisis, 42-52
    collapse of long-term capital management, 50
    justification for Islamic financial system-under economic crisis, 51-52
    primary cause of the crisis, 46-50
    prevailing imbalances in the U.S. economy, 50-51
HSBC, 39
HVB, 107

I

IAIB, 154
ICD, 111
ICT, 120
IDB, 26, 95, 99
IFSI, 42, 43, 143

IIBI in London, 152
Ijarah, 69-70
IMAGE, 173
IMUS, 40
International Holding Corporation, 114
International Monetary Fund, 18, 49, 51
Investment Committee Members, 80
IPOs, 125
Islam, 24, 90
Islamic Asset Management, 81
Islamic Bank, 52
Islamic finance, 3, 23-41
    definitions of Islamic economics, 26-27
    development and present condition, 38-41
    five prohibitions in financial activities in Islam, 28-29
    important principles of Islamic finance, 29-33
    interest free element in Islamic finance, 33-38
    profit and loss sharing principle, 41
    religious history of Islamic economics, 27-28
    what is Islamic finance, 24-26
    solution for global economic crisis, 1-3
Islamic Financial Services Board, 158
Islamic Financial System, 52
Islamic fund and asset management, 73-88
    financial ratios, 83
    Islamic funds and socially responsible investments, 78-80
    Islamic indexes for Islamic funds, 81-88
    Islamic unit trusts, 73-76
    leverage, 83-84
    monitoring fund documentation, 80
    parameters for acceptable industries, 81-82
    portfolio purification, 78-79
    proposed additional requirements for Islamic unit trust funds, 80-81
    revenue breakdown, 82-83
    review process for continued compliance, 88
    Shariah complaint equity funds Shariah perspective, 73
    Shariah principles for investment funds, 76-78
    working with fund management, 79
Islamic Institutions, 76
Islamic law, 54-55
Islamic law of contracts, 53-72
    classification of contract, 58-60
    contract of
        Ijarah, 69-70
        exchange, 61-69
        security, 70-72
    contracts of utilisation of usufruct, 69
    essential elements of a valid contract, 55-58
    historical evolution of contract in Islamic law, 54-55

reflection and overview on the classifications of contracts, 60-61

Islamic Unit Trust, 74

Ismail, Abul Halim, 38

K

Kafalah (bail/ suretyship), 72

KFH, 103

Khaleefa, 25

Kheiran Pearl City, 103

Khiyar (option), 64

KLSE Islamic Index, 88

KLSE National Shariah Index, 86, 88

Koran, 94

Kuala Lumpur Stock Exchange, 39

Kumpulan Guthrie Berhad, 105

L

Lease to Own, 118

LIBOR, 110

LLC, 121

LMC, 103

LP, 121

LTCM, 50

M

Majallah, 55

Malaysia Global Sukuk, 113

Malaysian Securities Commission, 80

Malikis, 58

MCCa, 153

Micro-Banking Bulletin, 174

Micro-finance institutions, 165

Micro-finance revolution, 166

Micro-finance, 160-174

boundaries and principles, 162-163

challenge, 160-162

current scale of micro-finance operations, 168-169

debates at the boundaries, 164-166

evidence for reducing poverty, 172-173

financial needs of poor people, 166-167

formal financial institutions, 171

inclusive financial systems, 169-170

informal financial service providers, 170

member-owned organizations, 170

micro-credit and the web, 172

micro-finance and social interventions, 173

NGOs, 171

other criticisms, 174

ways in which poor people manage their money, 167-168

Minute Maid, 123

MIT, 122

Mixed Islamic Fund, 78

Mortgage backed Securities, (MBS), 16

MS, 100

MTN, 95

Mudaraba, 41

Murabahah, 66

Musawamah, 66

Muslims, 80

N

National Bureau of Economic Research, 6

National Central Cooling Company, 110
National Venture Capital, 133
NGOs, 171
NVCA, 124

O

Ottoman Empire, 53

P

PBUH, 54
PLS, 136
Poverty Action/Financial Access Initiative Micro-Finance Research, 173

Q

Qatar Global Sukuk, 99
Quran, 24, 54

R

Rahn (pledges), 71-72
Risk Management Standards, 158
ROSCAs, 169
Rural banks, 168

S

SBA, 123
SBICs, 123
SCSI, 106
SEDC, 106
Shari'ah, 75
Shariah Committee, 78
Shariah principles for investment funds, 76-78
Shariah supervision in modern Islamic finance, 145-159
  background, 147
  elements of Shariah supervision, 147-148
    communication, 150
    education, 151
    independence, 150
    qualifications, 148-150
  importance of shariah supervision in Islamic financial institutions, 153-156
  issues relating to the working of SSBs, 156-157
  purpose, 146-147
  role of central banks and regulatory bodies, 157-159
  shariah supervision then and now, 151-153
  what is shariah supervision, 145-146
Siddiqi, Rushdi, 81
SMEs, 134
Special Purpose Vehicle, 92
SPV, 102
SRI, 83
SSB, 155, 156
STSL, 111
Sukuk, 89-119
  basics of sukuk, 92-93
  benefits and features, 98-99
  DP world Sukuk, 115-116
  Dubai civil aviation authority sukuk, 114-115
  Dubai world sukuk, 115
  eligible assets, 95-96
  enforceability, 96
  features of ijarah sukuk, 104-105
  future, 96
  German sukuk, 113

hybrid sukuk in practice, 111
ijara sukuk in practice, 105-107
increasing interest, 95
Islamic bonds, 96-97
istisna sukuk in practice, 110-111
model of a classic sukuk structure, 94-95
mudaraba sukuk in practice, 101-103
musharaka sukuk in practice, 103-104
role of sharia advisors in sukuk, 93-94
salam sukuk in practice, 108-110
sukuk in the context of UK and Europe, 94
sukuks by the governments of Bahrain, Qatar and Malaysia, 113-114
types of sukuk, 99-101
what is sukuk, 97-98

T

Tawheed, 29
Tawliyyah, 67
TCIPO, 95
TCs, 99
TTM, 137

U

United Prosperity, 172
United States, 12
United Youth Development Organization, 172
US Labour Department, 124
US Treasury Bonds, 141

V

VCs, 120, 128
Venrock Associates, 123
Venture capital, 120-144
bursting of the internet bubble and the private equity crash, 126-127
compensation, 130
conventional venture capital practice shariah view, 140-141
early venture capital and the growth of silicon valley, 123-124
establishment of the VC sector in the Islamic world, 133-137
history, 121-122
main alternatives to venture capital, 132-133
models and acceptable structures for Islamic venture capital, 137-140
origins of modern private equity, 122-123
roles within venture capital firms, 128-129
structure of the funds, 129-130
structure of venture capital firms, 127
structuring issues, 141-142
types of venture capital firms, 127-128
upsurge of Islamic syndicated financing, 142-144
venture capital boom and the internet bubble, 125-126

venture capital funding, 131-132
venture capital in the 1980s, 125
VLCC, 114

W

Wadiah, 67
World bank, 19, 22
World Competitiveness Report, 5
World Economic Outlook, 22, 49
World War II, 1
World War II, 9, 161, 122

Y

Yunus, Muhammad, 174